Tokyo T Guide Insiders

The Ultimate Travel Guide with Essential Tips About What to See, Where to Go, Eat, and Sleep even if Your Budget is Limited

>> ———————— <<

Contents

Discovering the City of Tokyo and Mount Fuji

Introduction to Japan

》》 ———————————— 《《

Japan is a nation where the past meets the future. Also referred to as Nihon or Nippon in Japanese, this island nation in East Asia has a history going back to before 300 BC and you can be sure that this country has seen it all. Very few nations in the world have such a colorful history as Japan. Dating back to the prehistoric era and seeing the rise and fall of countless emperors, the rule of the samurai warriors, and the isolation from the outside world for over 200 years, the Japanese take pride in having a rich history that you will certainly enjoy learning. Although Japan was one of the most warlike nations in the early 20th century, this has since changed and now it serves as a voice of pacifism and restraint on the international stage.

Japan also happens to be one of the countries that have experienced some of the biggest disasters, including the World War II atomic bombs, raging fires lasting for months, earthquakes, tsunamis, and typhoons just to mention some. The capital of Japan is Tokyo, which boasts of being the world's most populous metropolitan area with over 36 million residents.

The culture of Tokyo stretches back over a millennium, but it is also famous for adopting and creating the latest trends and fashions. If you are educated in the West, Japan can be a difficult country to understand and it can appear to be full of contradictions. It is dominated by Japanese corporations, but if you read the financial news, it may appear as though the country is practically bankrupt. While many cities are as high tech and modern as anywhere else, you can still spot tumbledown wooden shacks next to glass-fronted designer condominiums.

In the midst of modern skyscrapers, you will discover sliding wooden doors leading to traditional chambers with shoji screens, tatami mats, and calligraphy, ideal for traditional tea ceremonies. You may find these juxtapositions jarring or perplexing if you are used to the more uniform nature of North American or European cities, but if you clear your mind, start afresh, and acknowledge the layered aesthetics, you will find surprising and interesting places throughout the country.

The West has always identified Japan as a land that combines tradition and modernity. While many traditional practices and structures are preserved, modern practices and structures will certainly dominate your experience of the country. Japan was the first country in Asia to modernize independently and it continues to embrace new aesthetics and technologies. Even so, unlike many other nations, Japan does not seem to have any need to attack or remove older practices, structures, or technologies, and new things are structured next to old things. This does not necessarily mean that the country embraces massive preservation of historical structures or that the citizens generally practice traditional ceremonies. Nonetheless, Japanese people tend to believe that even if a small part of the population wants to preserve a building or continue a tradition, it should be respected. As such, development often takes place in a piecemeal fashion with one building at a time instead of large redevelopment projects, and you will often find that several urban blocks have evolved to align dozens of narrow buildings that cover fifty or more years of design history.

The History of Japan

Pre-historic Japan

It is highly likely that Paleolithic people first occupied Japan 35,000 years ago from the Asian mainland. About ten thousand years ago, at the end of the last Ice Age, a culture known as the Jomon was developed (DNA analyses suggest that the Ainu people could be the descendants of the

Jomon). The Jomon people were hunters, fishermen, and gatherers. They also made elaborate clay vessels, wooden houses, and fur clothing.

The Yayoi people came for the second wave of settlement at around 400 BC and introduced weaving, rice cultivation, and metalworking. DNA evidence suggests that the origin of these settlers was Korea.

In one of the accounts from the third century AD, a queen by the name of Himiko is mentioned in a Chinese historical document.

Kofun Period (300-710 AD)

In the 4th century, the ancestors of the present-day imperial family established the very first unified state in Japan under the Yamato court.

After the Yayoi people came the Kofun era, which is the first era of recorded history in the country to be characterized by tumuli, or large burial mounds – tombs made for the political class of the time. Also, within this period, agricultural tools, weapons, and other articles were introduced from Korea and China, led by a class of aristocratic warlords who adopted several Chinese innovations and customs.

Asuka Period (538-710 AD)

During this period, Buddhism was introduced to Japan, as well as the Chinese writing system. The society was grouped into clans, with the Yamato province as the headquarters.

Nara Period (710-794 AD)

The first stable central government was established in this period, including a Chinese system of law codes called the Ritsuryo system. Buddhism was the national religion and the people practiced Buddhist architecture and art. It was also during this time that the government constructed provincial temples referred to as kokubun-ji. One of the temples constructed during the era was the Todai-ji temple, which saw the building of the Great Buddha. For the most part, the aristocratic class practiced Buddhism while the agricultural villagers adopted Shintoism. It was around this time that the Chinese began to practice calligraphy.

It was also during the Nara period that the Man'yoshu was developed – a collection of the histories of Japan including Kojiki and Nihon Shoki.

Heian Period (794-1185 AD)

The unique culture of Japan developed quickly between 794 and 1185 during the Heian era. The imperial court turned out enduring prose, poetry, and art. The capital moved to what is now Kyoto, and some families started gaining government control to the extent of ruling on behalf of the emperor. At this time, the existing Chinese-style culture began to be replaced by an indigenous style of culture that was closer to the lives of the people and their surroundings. Palaces of the emperor and residents of noble families began incorporating beautiful gardens with different buildings – what is referred to as the Shiden-zukuri style of architecture. It was also during this period that some of the literary masterpieces like Murasaki Shikibu's *The Tale of Genji* were written.

The Kamakura Period (1185-1333 AD)

In the late Heian period, the Taira family, a warrior family with substantial control over the imperial court, was overthrown by the Minamoto family and Minamoto no Yoritoso was given the title of shogun by the court. The years following saw him set up a military-style government at Kakakura, forming the Kamakura Shogunate. This ushered in a period of military style of leadership. The artists of the time started embracing the warrior spirit as well to keep up with the times. Statues that were made included those of fierce guardian deities by sculptors like Unkei and others. Most of these were in the Southern Great Gate of the Todai-ji temple. Literature wasn't left behind; military stories like The Tale of the Heike were crafted to celebrate the success of the warriors.

Muromachi Period (1333-1568 AD)

This period was marred by political conflict between Emperor Go-Daigo and Ashikaga Takauji, his former supporter. The emperor restored some government control to the imperial court while Ashikaga Takauji overthrew the Kamakura Shogunate and established the Muromachi Shogunate, but the shogunate weakened due to substantial loss of control to the local warlords. The latter years of this period are often called the Sengoku period, which means warring states.

This period also marked the emergence of more plebeian forms of culture as peasants and merchants improved their circumstances. It was during this time that Chinese-style ink painting started taking root while in theater the Kyogen and the Noh drama started taking root. Tea ceremonies also increased in popularity and the culture of flower arrangement was born. In terms of architecture, the Shoin-zukuri style was born, which had beautiful tatami-matted rooms that featured an alcove where different paintings were hung.

The Azuchi-Momoyama Period (1568-1600 AD)

During this period, Toyotomi Hideyoshi and Oda Nobunaga unified the nation – these two were the foremost among the different Sengoku warlords. The period also saw increased contact with Europeans who started influencing art. The people started embracing a lavish decorative style in place of the Buddhist style and the new style was at its peak in Osaka Castle, Hideyoshi Castle, and Nobunaga's Azuchi Castle. The tea ceremony was officially traditionalized by tea master Sen no Rikyū, and this was referred to as the Way of Tea.

The Edo Period (1600-1868 AD)

The Tokugawa Shogunate was established in Edo (where Tokyo lies today) after Tokugawa Ieyasu defeated the other vassals during the battle of Sekigahara following the death of Toyotomi Hideyoshi. A famous Shinto shrine called Toshogu was built in 1617 in Nikko as a lavish memorial for Tokugawa Ieyasu as well as the site of his mausoleum. Nikko National Park is around two and a half hours north of Tokyo and certainly worth a visit if you're interested in this particular part of Japanese history. The Tokugawa shoguns ruled Japan for more than 260 years. During this period, Japan was literally shut off from foreign contact for about 200 years since the shogunate had a policy of national seclusion.

A new culture of artistic expression and economic activity developed at end of the 17th century and the beginning of the 18th century, especially among the townspeople of older cities like Osaka and Kyoto. It was during this period that Ihara Saikaku composed the *Ukiyo-zoshi* (the books of the floating world). There was also Chikamatsu Monzaemon who portrayed different tragic relationships between women and men through puppet plays. Printing of books started taking root in the shogun capital of Edo (now Tokyo). Woodblock print (Ukiyo-e) was established, which saw the production of portraits of different actors.

The Meiji Period (1868-1912 AD)

During the Meiji restoration, political authority was restored back to the imperial court from the shogunate. The national seclusion policy also ended and a new culture and civilization (Western culture) started taking root. There was also the birth of modern Japanese literature including Futabatei Shimei's novel *Ukigumo*, which means Drifting Clouds.

The other periods were the Taisho Period (1912-1926), the Showa period (1926-1989), and the modern period. All these paint a story of how Japan grew from a prehistoric country to a modern society that boasts of being a nation that has risen from the ashes.

Things You Should Know Before You Travel to Japan

»» —————————— ««

Respect and How to Address Someone

For Japanese people, bowing is nothing less than a form of art, a form of respect taught to children from the moment they enter school. For tourists, an attempt of a bow at the waist, or a simple inclination of the head will suffice. The level of inclination and the duration will depend on the person you are addressing. A friend, for instance, may get a lightning-fast thirty degree bow, while an office superior might receive a slow and extended seventy degree bow. It is all about circumstance and position.

Apart from bowing, addressing a person in the right manner is equally important. It's just the same as a certain "Dr. James" may feel slightly insulted if you were to refer to him as simply "James", and similarly would a Japanese person if you failed to include the suffix "san" after their last name, or if you are trying to be especially respectful, "sama". Children are usually content with just their first names, but if you like, you could add the suffix "kun" for boys and "chan" for girls.

Table Manners

If you are at a dinner party and happen to receive drinks, do not rush to raise the glass to your lips. Everyone is bound to be served, and someone will take the lead, present a speech, raise his drink, and then exclaim "kampai!" which essentially means "cheers!" Most Japanese restaurants will normally give you a small wet cloth. Use this to wash your hands before you eat, then fold it carefully and set it aside on the table. Do not touch it on any part of your face or use it as a napkin.

It is okay to make loud noises and slurp noodles while eating. Surprisingly, slurping hot foods, such as ramen is considered polite to show that you are enjoying it. You are also allowed to raise the bowl to your mouth when using chopsticks in order to make it easier eat, especially for bowls of rice. Right before you dig in, whether it is a sample at a supermarket or a seven-course dinner, it is considered polite to say" itadakimasu", which simply means "I will receive."

No Tipping

You are not allowed to tip in any situation in Japan, including personal care, restaurants, and cabs. In fact, it is considered slightly insulting to tip someone. The price you paid covered the service requested, so why pay more?

If you are in a large city like Tokyo and you cannot speak any Japanese, a waitress or waiter may take the extra money you happen to leave in order to avoid the awkward situation of having to explain the concept that there is no tipping in broken English. Just keep in mind that a price is a price.

Chopsticks

Depending on the restaurant, you might be required to use chopsticks. If you are not familiar with using chopsticks, try to learn before you enter the country. In case you happen to dine with a Japanese person, do not be surprised by their amazement at your ability to use chopsticks well.

Thresholds

Be sure to take off your shoes at the entrance to most hotels and businesses, and all homes. A rack will usually be provided to place your shoes along with a pair of guest slippers. However, many Japanese carry a pair of indoor slippers just in case. Avoid using slippers when stepping onto a tatami mat (used in many Japanese hotels and homes), and be careful to wear the right slippers for each separate space. For instance, it would not be proper to enter the main room of a house again while wearing the same slippers you were using across dirty linoleum.

Masks

Even before the pandemic, sterilized masks such as those you would see in an emergency room were used popularly by municipal workers as well as office workers to prevent other people from contracting their germs. When you think about it, it is rather sensible considering the fact that masks do not really protect the wearers so much as those around them. It could be for fear of spreading a potential cold or simply out of consideration for the health and safety of others.

Conformity

If groups of Japanese students are asked to identify the risks facing children today, the majority of them would agree on one thing: individualism. Japanese society is focused on the group while Western cultures are centered on the individual. Does this mean that the Japanese people are merely worker bees in a vast hive of concrete and steel? Of course not, but exhibition of individual characteristic is calculated carefully and provided in small doses, and it is not acceptable to draw attention to yourself as an individual. Do not talk on the phone in crowded public areas such as buses or trains, avoid eating as much as possible while on the go, and do not blow your nose in public. The issue with this is that foreigners simply cannot avoid standing out. You may stick out like a sore thumb no matter how many times you have been to Japan or how much you know about their culture and society.

For this reason, being in Japan tends to give foreigners the rank of D-level celebrities. You may get shouts for attention, glances, and calls to have pictures taken with the locals, and even requests for autographs.

Bathing

There are active and lively bathhouses in Japan. You can find neighborhood bathhouses, or sento, from a small town on the island of Shikoku to the businest location in Shinjuku. Hot springs, or onsen, are extremely popular as weekend getaways. Unlike in Western culture, you are supposed to bathe after you have washed and rinsed and just enjoy soaking in hot water for ten to thirty minutes. It is an acquired taste but can be very relaxing. In case you are invited to a Japanese household, the honor of having the bath first will be given to you, normally before dinner. Be sure not to make the water dirty in any way. The sacredness of the bath, or ofuro, is of utmost importance. If you have the chance, find some time to visit a sento. These are places with no barriers, with no regard for language, age, or skin color; well, they are divided by sex, except for a few mixed bathing areas.

Speaking English

Until you prove otherwise, Japanese people will generally assume that you are a native speaker of English. Even during a short visit, you may experience a random person walking up to you and asking where you are from. This may seem friendly and interesting at first, but it is easy to see how the constant celebrity status can be frustrating or confusing for travelers who do not speak English.

Although you may speak a little or even fluent Japanese, the preferred default language to converse with foreigners is English and most Japanese people will likely insist on using English to speak with you, however limited their ability, even if you may know the local tongue.

Safety

Japan is a very safe country, but it is still advisable to be careful in your travels and to take care of your belongings. The fear of crime is very high in Japan, especially among Japanese citizens, and although generally safe, crimes do occur, including violent ones, and there is also organized crime. Overall, Japan has a low crime rate and you may sometimes spot businessmen sleeping on park benches after missing the last train.

Shibuya

First of all, where is Shibuya?

Geographically, Shibuya occupies the southwest side of central Tokyo and it can be found on the famous Yamanote Line, a train rail that goes around and around on the perimeter of Chiyoda Ward where you can find the Imperial Palace and its gigantic gardens. In fact, Yamanote Line tends to be where the tired businessmen occasionally take their late night naps, so that after a few rounds they can go back to work without having to return home at all.

Just to give you an idea about the extremely high number of train and metro lines that enmesh the metropolis, here is a list of the main ones going through Shibuya, which is a popular destination for both tourists and locals – Metro: Ginza Line, Hanzomon Line, and Fukutoshin Line; Train: JR Yamanote Line, JR Chuo Line, JR Saikyo Line, Keio Inokashira Line, Tokyu Toyoko Line, Tokyu Denentoshi Line, and Tokyu Setagaya Line. Of course, there are many more that pass very close to central Shibuya.

What should you know about Shibuya?

According to one of the theories, this area used to be an inlet and was called the "Village of Salt Valley" (Shioya no Sato). This "Shioya" later changed to "Shibuya" and this name has remained until today. One would have to go back all the way to the prehistoric ages to find the first known dwellers. Much later during the Muromachi Period (1336-1573), a village began to form here and kept growing until the establishment of Tokyo in 1868. Finally, in 1932, the current borders were drawn after countless mergers and separations.

What else?

The current population is about 250 thousand people; however, during daytime this number increases to about 600 thousand. Most of the citizens live alone, unmarried, and rent an apartment, as opposed to buying one. Many of them seem to leave after a while, but as there are new ones moving in right away, the actual population of the ward does not change that much. It is a place where everyone would love to live at least once in a lifetime before they settle down somewhere else. Approximately 350 thousand people come here to work every day, and there are over 32 thousand offices (27% in the retail industry) to employ them.

Shibuya is one of the most popular and easily accessible places to work. Central Shibuya has been evolving at an incredible speed. A project to re-develop the Shibuya Station and its vicinity is ongoing and Shibuya Hikarie, a cultural and business center, was completed first in 2012 as a part of this project. Construction of the station's East Tower completed in 2019, making it the tallest station in all of Japan at 230 meters. By 2027, work on the West Tower and the Central Tower will be also finished. Moreover, they built a big bus terminal near the towers to connect directly to the airport. Finally, in the southern part of this area, Shibuya River will emerge once again, surrounded by a relaxing park.

What is near the station?

Besides the thousands of workplaces and six universities (by the way, there are around 150 universities and colleges in the 23 Special Wards of Tokyo, which is at least twice as many as in Boston, London, or Beijing), what makes so many people want to visit or live here?

The answer is the social/night life and entertainment. Every day, hundreds and hundreds of people wait for their friends or co-workers near the Hachiko Statue in front of the northern Hachiko Gate of the station. This statue was built in memory of a dog, Hachiko, who, even after his owner had passed away, kept waiting for him every day for 9-10 years at the Shibuya Station.

The owner was a professor named Ueno Hidesaburo at the Agricultural Department of the former Imperial University of Tokyo, who suddenly died in 1925. In 2015, around eighty years after the death of Hachiko, the staff of the Agricultural Department built a new statue with the professor and his dog standing together.

gotokyo.org

The first Hachiko statue was erected in Shibuya in 1934; however it was removed during World War II in the name of metal contribution, only to be reinstalled in 1948 after the end of the war.

Another favorite spot to meet is at the Moyai Statue near the Western Gate of the station. It was a present by Nii-jima (a volcanic island in the Philippine Sea) in 1980, celebrating the 100th anniversary of their administration being transferred to the Tokyo Government.

After meeting up with someone in front of the Hachiko Statue, you must follow the crowd to the famous crossing where roughly 3,000 people cross at each green light.

Once you have sort of bobbed to the other side of the street in a wave of people, you may come realize that it will not be easy to choose where to eat or drink: within the vicinity of the main station, there are hundreds of bars, restaurants, and cafés. The most popular izakayas (Japanese style pubs) are:

MIRAIZAKA

Dogenzaka Center Bldg. 5F, Dogenzaka 2-29-8, Shibuya-ku
Phone: +81-50-2019-7272
Hours: 17:00-3:00 (weekdays), 16:00-3:00 (weekends and the day before any national holiday)

Doma-Doma

Address: Kaleido Shibuya Miyamasuzaka 6F, Shibuya 1-12-1, Shibuya-ku, Tokyo
Phone: +81 3-5778-9650
Hours: 17:00-4:30 (weekdays), 14:00-4:30 (weekends)

For something more special, for example a date, *CÉ LA VI* is recommended, where you can gaze at the illuminated city at night from a 17th or 18th floor lounge.

CÉ LA VI

Address: Tokyu Plaza Shibuya 17-18F, Dogenzaka 1-2-3,
Shibuya-ku, Tokyo
Phone: +81-3-5422-3137
Hours: 11:00-17:00 lunch & tea, 19:00-23:00 dinner

If it is sushi that you are looking for, at *Zauo* you can catch your own fish, which, once you actually succeed in doing so, the staff will prepare for you to eat.

Zauo Shibuya

Address: Hymanten Jinnan Bldg. B1, Jinnan 1-19-3,
Shibuya-ku, Tokyo
Phone: +81-3-6427-0207
Hours: 17:00-23:00 (weekdays), 11:30-23:00 (weekends and national holidays)

There is of course a much more relaxed way to eat sushi, especially if the food is carried to you on conveyer belts:

Katsumidori Seibu Shibuya

Address: A-Bldg. 8F Food Mall Dining Plaza, Udagawa-cho 21-1, Shibuya-ku, Tokyo
Phone: +81-3-5728-4282
Hours: 11:00-22:00 every day

In case the occasion demands a more formal setting, you are sure to impress your guests at *Seiryu Hatsu-tsubomi*.

Seiryu Hatsu-tsubomi

Address: Shibuya Square Bldg. A-Wing B1, Dogenzaka 1-9-5, Shibuya-ku, Tokyo
Phone: +81-3-3463-2284
Hours: 11:30-22:00 (weekdays), 16:00-22:00 (weekends)

If you're in the mood to sing, you can choose from over 20 karaoke places. The most popular are *Big Echo*, *Utahiroba*, and *Karaoke-kan* as they tend to have the biggest selection of songs at affordable prices. If you want to go shopping, there are over 200 retail stores on Dogenzaka Street alone, which is the main street of Shibuya Center-Gai.

A brief history of Center-Gai

Construction started along the shores of Uda River in 1929 and restaurants and cafés began to pop up after 1935. The river used to flood after heavy rain causing trouble for these establishments. Right before the 1964 Tokyo Olympics, Uda River became an under-drain to allow for more surface area to build on. In 1973, Center-Gai reached its current form with the famous arch.

In 2011, this area was (unfortunately) renamed "Basketball Street" to change its image to be more international, healthy, and energetic. Another reason could be because the biggest basketball store in Japan is on this street (*GALLERY 2*).

One of the main symbols of Center-Gai is *Shibuya 109*, a large shopping mall with many female apparel stores. It was built by Tokyu Group, which owns many train lines within Tokyo. The name came from a play on words: 109 can be read as "to" (ten) and "kyu" (nine) in Japanese. On weekends or holidays, it has an average of 35 thousand visitors a day, from which we can estimate the great influence it has on the contemporary clothing trends among women and teenage girls. Besides their clothing chains within Japan, they also opened their first store in Hong Kong in 2015.

If you like cigars and want to take a break, you can check out *R261 Cigar & Rock* just west of the station for a great selection of cigars and drinks in a relaxing atmosphere.

R261 Cigar & Rock

Address: Cerulean Tower Tokyu Hotel 2F, Sakuragaoka-cho 26-1, Shibuya-ku, Tokyo
Phone: +81-3-3476-3526
Hours: 16:00-23:00 (Sun-Mon), 16:00-24:00 (Fri-Sat)

If you are bored with shopping, eating, drinking, smoking, or singing, you can visit the local cinema plaza (*Toho Cinemas*), the *Taito Game* arcades to take purikura (explanation later), the bowling and billiard area at *Shibuya EST*, or just walk around and take in the street art while listening to sidewalk jam sessions. If you are lucky, you might discover a few art pieces by the famous Japanese artist, 281_Anti nuke.

roomie.jp

If you enjoy playing more serious sports, you can reserve a futsal court for you and your friends at the *Adidas Futsal Park* on the 4th floor of *Shibuya Steam*, a skyscraper and retail complex, or even join a tournament. Look up *Adidas Futsal Park* for up-to-date information on latest events. You can also check out their website for details: https://www.tokyu-sports.com/football/reyes/adidas_futsal_park/shibuya.html

What is "purikura", you ask?

The name comes from "Print Club", a series of fun self-shot machines created by Atlus Company in 1995, which became extremely popular in the end of the 90's. Now, there are many other companies producing purikura machines and they are quite common to visit after eating out and drinking with friends/co-workers, even for adults. By the way, the biggest purikura store in Japan is also in Shibuya, equipped with as many as 17 machines (*Purikura Shop NOA*).

If you are a music lover, *Shibuya Club Quattro* is highly recommended. Here you can see both local and international artists in a relatively small arena, where the stage is just an arm's length away (for the schedule, visit http://www.club-quattro.com/shibuya/schedule/). If you happen to miss the last train after all the fun activities (which happens more frequently than you would imagine), don't worry. You can always stay at one of the manga kissas (manga cafés) near the station where you rent a tiny private cubicle with a computer and a couch/bed. You can spend the night for 2-3 thousand yen, while reading as many manga as you want, watching movies, or surfing the net. Of course, you are more than welcome to sleep as well, if you feel like it. Once you have discovered Central Shibuya, it is time to venture out a bit more into the diverse neighborhoods.

Harajuku

You can simply walk (15 minutes) or take the JR Yamanote Line (2 minutes, 140 yen) from Shibuya. During the Edo Period, this area was full of samurai residences. In the Meiji Period, noblemen lived here. In 1964, Tokyo Olympics was partly (swimming, basketball, etc.) held at Yoyogi National Gymnasium, which is only a few minutes away.

After the opening of *Mademoiselle Nonnon* boutique in 1966, Harajuku became the fashion and youth (sub) culture center of Tokyo. You can find teenagers representing various styles: kawaii, lolita goth, cosplay, etc., especially on Takeshita-dori, one of the most lively shopping streets in Tokyo. You should also visit Harajuku-dori and Shibuyagawa-hodoro (nickname: Cat Street), collectively called "Urahara" (literally: back side of Harajuku), where you can find the smaller shops that could not afford to open on the expensive Takeshita-dori.

Meiji Shrine

After visiting Harajuku, you can make your way towards the Meiji Shrine, which can be approached directly from the JR Harajuku Station in a few minutes. In this shrine, Emperor Meiji and Empress Shoken are worshipped. Its peaceful and breathtaking forest consists of approximately 10 thousand trees, which were donated from all over the country.

The forest has grown into a 70 thousand square meter area, providing the visitors not only with a calming atmosphere but also with many sport and museum facilities as well as a gorgeous location for weddings. This shrine receives most of its visitors at New Year's during hatsu-mode or hatsu-mairi, which is generally done right after midnight, but can extend until the 3rd day of January. This is when they thank the gods for the past year and pray for the success and happiness of the New Year.

The number of people visiting here during the first 3 days of the New Year is more than 3 million. The shrine is open from 5-6:00 to 17-18:00 (depending on the season). The garden, which includes flowers originally planted by the emperor as a present to the empress, opens a bit later and closes a bit earlier, and can be observed for 500 yen. After visiting the main shrine building, you should keep walking north until you reach a museum called Homotsuden where you can find many personal items of the emperor and the empress, as well as temporary exhibitions. It is usually open from 9:00 until 16:00 and the entrance fee is 500 yen.

In Japan, there are generally three types of weddings: kyokai-shiki, shinzen-shiki, and jinzen-shiki. Kyokai-shiki is a Christian inspired church wedding involving wearing a typical white wedding dress and a black suit regardless of whether or not the couple is Christian. Shinzen-shiki is a wedding in a Shinto shrine wearing a kimono, whereas jinzen-shiki has no limitation concerning location or clothes. In Japan, there is a growing tendency to have a kyokai-shiki wedding due to Western cultural influence.

Yoyogi Park

The southern part of this gigantic green area is called Yoyogi Park, where the Olympic Village used to be in 1964. It is a perfect spot for a picnic, to play sports, or to hang out with friends. This green space full of ponds, fountains, and trees is currently the fifth biggest of its kind within the 23 Special Wards. You can also visit the only remaining house from the Olympic Village where a Dutch athlete used to stay. From time to time, there are international beer/gourmet festivals and flea markets in this park.

Omotesando

This is an area between Shibuya and Harajuku, slightly to the east. The main walking street, Aoyama-dori, extends from Omotesando Station all the way to Shibuya Station. Omotesando has been formed by the contrast between the traditional Japanese atmosphere of Meiji Shrine and its antonym Harajuku, which is a hub for Western culture.

However, unlike Harajuku, the main influence here has been foreign cuisine, especially French. As such, you can find the biggest variety of French cuisine here. There are also quite a few Italian, Spanish, and Central European restaurants in the area. I would recommend the Austrian *Cafe Landtmann* for dinner and the French *Glaciel Omotesando* for dessert.

Cafe Landtmann

Address: Ao Bldg. 4F, Kita-aoyama 3-11-7, Minato-ku, Tokyo

Phone: +81 50-5486-3659

Hours: 11:00-23:00 (Mon – Sat), 11:00-22:00 (Sun and national holidays)

Glaciel Omotesando

Address: 5th SI Bldg. 1F, Kita-aoyama 3-6-26, Minato-ku

Phone: +81-3-6427-4666

Hours: 12:00-19:00

Qu'il fait bon down the street (4-minute walk) is also a great choice for dessert if you feel like trying their famous tarts.

Qu'il fait bon

Address: Minami-aoyama 3-18-5, Minato-ku, Tokyo

Phone: +81-3-5414-7741

Hours: 11:00 to 19:00

Daikanyama

This is a gorgeous neighborhood in the southern part of the Shibuya Ward. You can get there from central Shibuya by using the Tokyu Toyoko Line (3 minutes, 130 yen) or on foot (17 minutes). Almost every weekend, there are food and handicraft markets on the two main streets: Kyuu-Yamate-dori and Hachiman-dori. Daikanyama is the perfect place to arrange business or academic meetings – it is beautifully and simply designed and also calm and quiet, making it easy to hold conversations. The most beautiful *Tsutaya* store is also located here.

Tsutaya began in Osaka City in 1983 as a book, music, and movie retail shop, and over the years it began to operate as a movie rental as well. However, the youth of the time grew up and *Tsutaya* decided to dedicate the Daikanyama store to them with a more mature theme. It has won the grand prize at the 2012 World Architecture Festival in the Best Shopping Center category, and also at the 2012 Design for Asia (most prestigious design award in Asia). It has also been included in "The 20 Most Beautiful Bookstores in the World" list by Flavorwire, a popular NY-based cultural website. It opened in 2011 and is usually referred to as "T-Site". There are many temporary exhibitions here as well as talks with artists and academicians (for more information: https://tsite.jp/).

Ebisu

From Shibuya Station, walk south for 13 minutes or take the Shonan-Shinjuku line to Ebisu (2 min, 140 yen). Northwest of the station, there is a statue of Ebisu, the Japanese god of fishermen, a popular meeting spot like the Hachiko statue. A bit south of the station, there is *Museum of Yebisu Beer* and *Tokyo Photographic Art Museum* (technically in Meguro).

Museum of Yebisu Beer

Address: Yebisu Garden Place, Ebisu 4-20-1, Shibuya-ku
Phone: +81-3-5423-7255
Hours: 11:00-19:00 (closed on Mon) (free entry)

Tokyo Photographic Art Museum

Address: Yebisu Garden Place, Mita 1-13-3, Meguro-ku
Phone: +81-3-3280-0099
Hours: 10:00-18:00 (closed Mon) (1000 yen for entry)

Meguro

If you went to *Tokyo Photographic Art Museum*, you are already in the northern tip of Meguro. Head a bit southwest to the Meguro River Cherry Blossoms Promenade, which is particularly stunning during the spring bloom season (hanami – more details later). If you are interested in the history of

Meguro, there is the Meguro History Museum nearby (9:30-17:00 Tue-Sun, free entry). Depending on your interests, you can find to the south *Meguro Museum of Art* (10:00-18:00 Tue-Sun, 800 yen) and *Meguro Parasitological Museum*, a small medical museum devoted to parasites (10:00-17:00 Wed-Sun, free entry). There is also *Hotel Gajoen Tokyo*, a luxury hotel where you can find lodging as well as special exhibitions (https://www.hotelgajoen-tokyo.com/).

Shimokitazawa

A bit west of Shibuya is Shimokitazawa (or Shimo-Kitazawa), also known as Shimokita. Take the Keio Inokashira line from Shibuya Station to Shimo-Kitazawa (6 min, 130 yen). This area is famous for its vintage clothing stores, independent bookstores, music and novelty shops supporting local artists, small galleries, craft cafés and pubs, theaters, and live music venues. There are so many different kinds of trendy and unique shops and venues here that you are sure to find something that delights you! This area is also full of excellent Japanese curry restaurants, notable among which are *Rojiura Curry Samurai* and *Magic Spice*.

Shinjuku

»» ———————————— ««

A quick history lesson about Shinjuku

Now that you know where Shibuya is, you will have no problem finding Shinjuku as it is located only 3 stations to the north of Shibuya on the Yamanote Line (7 minutes, 160 yen). Its name comes from the 17th century (Edo Period), when a certain number of lodgings ("yado" or "shuku" in Japanese) were required for each of the five main roads ("kaido") running through the country. On the Koshu-kaido, the first lodging after Nihombashi (the beginning point of all the five roads, located in Edo/Tokyo) was a bit too far; therefore the local village leader requested a closer one to be built. It was called Naito-Shinjuku as it was placed inside the Naito clan's premises ("shin" means "new" in Japanese, and "juku" is just "shuku," but voiced). The train station opened in 1885, and the ward itself was created by merging some areas around the main station in 1947 and it was named after the station. The area suffered great damage in 1945 during the Great Tokyo Air Raid when 90% of the houses were destroyed and its population declined to 20% of the original 400 thousand. Since then, however, the ward has seen modernization and development to an incredible extent.

After the Tokyo Metropolitan Government headquarters moved here from Marunouchi in 1991, this area became the so-called "new center" of Tokyo. Most of the people from outside the 23 Special Wards come here to work, thus Shinjuku serves as a bridge between central and western Tokyo, making it the most active area in Japan. Projections show that its daytime population is well over 800 thousand, which would make it the most crowded ward in the capital. No wonder, then, that most of the foreigners in Tokyo live here as well, with around 45 thousand registered.

This ward has the biggest density of malls, *McDonald's*, and *Uniqlo's* in all of Japan. You must have heard of *Uniqlo* already, although perhaps you did not know that it is from Japan. *Uniqlo* is a clothing apparel company founded in 1949 in Yamaguchi Prefecture. Currently, they have as many as 2,400 stores worldwide. Their heat-tech undershirts and underpants go a long way towards helping you survive the freezing cold winters of Tokyo.

The station and its crepes!

Shinjuku Station opened in 1885 and is currently the busiest station in the world according to the Guinness Book of World Records, with over 3.6 million passengers per day. Before we move on to our next destination, first you must try the delicious crepes around the station.

&.Shinjuku (crepe and coffee shop)

Address: Shinjuku Mylord Mosaic Street, Nishishinjuku 1-1-3
Phone: +81-80-7470-7635
Hours: 11:00-21:00 (check out https://and-coffee.jp/)

Crepe Petit Varie

Address: Kirin Bldg. 1F, Shinjuku 3-36, Shinjuku-ku, Tokyo
Phone: +81-3-3226-3788
Hours: 12:00-23:00

Shinjuku Gyoen

Another namesake of the ward is Shinjuku Gyoen, a national garden that opened in 1906. The mansion of the Naito clan used to be here during the Edo Period. Although it was designed as a garden for the imperial family, it was opened to the public after World War II. Within its approximately 58-hectare area, there is a Japanese garden, an English-style landscape garden, and a French-style plane-geometrical garden. There are also over 1,300 cherry trees, which makes it an ideal place for hanami (you can find more details about this in the chapter about Ueno) in the beginning of April. Between November 1 and 15, you can also enjoy the view of the beautiful chrysanthemums, which are the symbol of the imperial family (you may remember this from the title of Ruth Benedict's book, *The Chrysanthemum and the Sword*). It is generally open between 9:00 and 16:00, and the entry fee is 500 yen. It is only 10 minutes by walk from Shinjuku Station.

Let's go to the Tokyo Toy Museum!

This is a three-story building with over 10,000 toys for both children and their parents to enjoy from about 100 different countries. The staff is there to help you to figure out how to play with them. There are toy making workshops throughout the week (free on weekdays and 1,000 yen on weekends).

Entry costs 1,100 yen for adults. Remember to bring some onigiri with you for lunch (rice ball with some sort of filling) so that you can spend the whole day playing! Before visiting, be sure to make a reservation at: https://art-play.or.jp/ttm/

Tokyo Toy Museum

Address: Yotsuya Hiroba, Yotsuya 4-20, Shinjuku-ku, Tokyo
(6 minutes walk from Shinjuku Gyoen)
Phone: +81-3-5367-9601
Hours: 10:00-16:00 (closed Thu)

If you are still hungry, you can visit one of the *Go! Go! Curry* restaurants in Shinjuku, where they sell giant portions for affordable prices. There is also *Komoro Soba* for the more health-conscious people. Soba, by the way, is a thin noodle made from buckwheat flour, served with either cold or hot soup – very tasty, but to be honest, not quite as filling.

Takadanobaba

You can either walk here (32 minutes) or take the Yamanote Line from Shinjuku (5 minutes, 140 yen). The first thing you will see after leaving the station behind you is the *BIG BOX* building, which literally looks like a big box. It offers a great variety of sport activities for visitors such as bowling, swimming, and tennis.

As there are many universities and colleges nearby (e.g. Waseda University), you can find a satisfying selection of ramen stores among many other cheap food choices near the station.

Did you know that over 1,300 Myanmarese people live in this area? Frankly, I was quite surprised myself. They live in Little Yangon, north of the station, and their restaurants are most certainly worth a try.

You can also visit the Japan Braille Library (Nihon Tenji Toshokan, or Nitten for short), which was founded in 1940 by Honma Kazuo, a blind journalist and entrepreneur. If you notify them beforehand, a staff member will guide you around and show you the sound studio for the audio books as well as the braille production room. Check out their website for more information (https://www.nittento.or.jp/en/).

Kabuki-cho

If you are not yet exhausted from all the sightseeing and playing, you should definitely see the (in)famous nightlife in the red light and entertainment district, Kabuki-cho, which is just outside the Eastern Gate of Shinjuku Station. You will surely be able to find some of the strangest places here, from a restaurant where girls ride dancing/fighting robots to a bar filled with horror movie memorabilia, all the way to the extremely narrow "Memory Lane" (formerly known as "Piss Alley" – I suppose the reason for the name change is rather obvious), where you will soon forget about concepts such as personal space (if you have not already while riding the train/metro during rush hour).

Robot Restaurant

Address: Shinjuku Robot Bldg. B2F, Kabuki-cho 1-7-1, Shinjuku-ku, Tokyo
Phone: +81-50-5869-5074 (for reservations only)
Remark: The entrance fee is 8,500 yen and there are four performances every evening.

Unfortunately, Robot Restaurant closed due to the pandemic but may reopen in the future. Visit their website for updates (http://www.shinjuku-robot.com). In the meantime, try *Kujira Entertainment* for an immersive experience of music, shows, food, and drinks!

Kujira Entertainment

Address: Furin Kaikan B2, Kabuki-cho 2-23-1, Shinjuku-ku
Phone: +81-3-6205-6675
Hours: 21:00-05:00 (closed on Sunday)
Remarks: For details on prices and events, check out their website: https://kujiraentertainment.com

If you are in the mood for some okonomiyaki (Japanese pancake cooked on a teppan), try *Teppan Baby* where you'll find tiny plastic babies among the plates.

Teppan Baby

Address: Pocket Bldg. B1F, Kabuki-cho 1-17-4, Shinjuku-ku
Phone: +81 3-3204-1333
Hours: 17:00-05:00 (Mon-Sat), 17:00-00:00 (Sun)

For a change of pace, if you are interested in horror movies and heavy metal, you may feel right at home sipping a drink at *Deathmatch in Hell*, where most drinks cost 666 yen.

Deathmatch in Hell

Address: Golden Gai 3rd St., Kabuki-cho 1-1-8, Shinjuku-ku
Phone: +81 90-2524-5575
Hours: 20:00-03:00 Mon-Sat, closed on Sun and holidays (schedule may vary from week to week so be sure to check their Facebook page for updated information)

The Memory Lane (or Omoide-yokocho in Japanese) is easily accessible from the Eastern Gate of Shinjuku Station. Just walk towards the gigantic ALTA sign, then before crossing the street, enter a sketchy pedestrian underpass on your left, which will bring you directly to this tiny street with more than 80 bars and restaurants on it.

Ikebukuro

L et's go northwest on the Yamanote Line to reach the Ikebukuro Station. While the name of the station literally means "pound bag", in reality, the name originates from the old geographical feature of this land, where many lakes used to lie. So, in this case, "fukuro" means a land surrounded by water, and not a bag.

Due to the phonological similarity of the words bag and owl in Japanese (the former is "fukuro" and the latter "fukurō"), you will surely bump into quite a few owl-themed works of art, both inside and out- side the station. Among these, the most famous is a stone statue near the Eastern Gate, (very craftily) called "Ikefukurō". This is a major meeting point around here, much like the Hachiko Statue in front of Shibuya Station. It was installed in 1987 when Japan Railways (JR) was born, taking over Japanese National Railways through privatization.

Three baby owls were also recently added to the figure.

Ikebukuro area is home to the Kyokuto-kai, a peddler-type yakuza faction. There was even a Japanese TV show about them, *Ikebukuro West Gate Park*, which aired in 2000. The group was established in 1990 and currently has about 430 members.

Ikebukuro Sunshine City

In the center of Sunshine City stands a 239.7-meter tall skyscraper, Sunshine 60, which used to be the tallest building in Asia back when it was completed in 1978. Moreover, its indoor observatory, located on the 60th floor, was the highest of its kind until they built Tokyo Skytree in 2011. It also had an observatory on the roof; however, after two suicides it has been closed to the public. Since the 70's, an unbelievable number of facilities have been added around this building: offices and retail stores, a hotel, an aquarium, an indoor theme park (*Namja Town*), a planetarium, a theater, a convention hall, and even apartment buildings. According to the latest statistics, the center receives around 30 million visitors annually.

Namco, the same company that created the arcade game Pac-Man in 1980, possibly one of the most famous games ever, owns the attraction center *Namja Town*. Within *Namja Town*, among many other fun things, you can find food areas with various themes. *Gyoza Stadium* is the place to visit if you are looking for the best savory dumplings. Besides the regular gyoza filled with pork and vegetable, there are also ones containing seafood or cheese, for example. This does sound very exciting, but please make sure to leave some space in your second stomach ("betsubara" in Japanese) for a delicious and slightly shocking dessert experience. By the way, the mechanism of the second stomach has recently been investigated by a Japanese gastroenterologist, Koyama Shigeki, and his results show that the visual stimulus of a dessert can, in fact, cause the stomach to make room for the subsequent feast.

After sampling the gyoza, your next destination must be Fukubukuro Dessert Yokocho. Within this area, you will find cute and interesting dessert shops, often with many different flavors of ice cream, from which you can choose mix and match on your plate. Besides the run-of-the-mill apple or peach, you may find more unusual flavors like the lavender and tulip flavors. If you're feeling more adventurous, you can see about experimenting with flavors like miso ramen, eel, oyster, Hokkaido potato, and curry. Not wild enough for you? Ask about garlic and wasabi ice creams. Price starts from about 400 yen and can be higher depending on your choices.

The entrance fee into *Namja Town* is 500 yen for adults (although some attractions cost extra) and it is open between 10:00 and 21:00 (https://bandainamco-am.co.jp/tp/namja/).

Kit Kat Chocolatory

Not enough weird flavors? You might want to visit the *Kit Kat Chocolatory* inside the Seibu Ikebukuro Department Store. Japanese people are big fans of this snack, which might have something to do with the fact that Kit Kat sounds a bit like "kitto katsu", meaning "(I will) definitely win". Here you can stimulate your taste buds with purple potato, cinnamon cookie, cheese, bean, or wasabi flavored chocolates. And there's more. There are three special flavors developed by a Japanese chocolatier Takagi Yasumasa: Sublime Bitter, Special Sakura Green Tea, and Special Chili. Bon appetite!

Rikkyo University (St. Paul's University)

This is a private Christian university in west Ikebukuro, only a 10-minute walk from the station. Initially, they taught English and Bible Studies when it opened in 1874 as Rikkyo School. Channing Moore Williams, who was one of the first Christian missionaries visiting Japan in the 19th century, founded the school. Later, in 1866, he became the Episcopal missionary bishop for both Japan and China. The university has many beautiful buildings made out of red bricks. Unfortunately, it is usually closed to the public, but you can still sneak a peek from the outside. Or you can wait until August when they open their gates for prospective students.

Otsuka

This area is a 24-minute walk from Ikebukuro Station or a 2-minute ride on the Yamanote Line (140 yen). You will be surprised by how calm this neighborhood is, despite its proximity to the busy Ikebukuro.

You will probably also notice that you can actually breathe in some fresh air here and move around without colliding with anyone. The perfect time to visit is at sunset when the orange lights so breathtakingly emphasize the nostalgic streets and little shops. It is as if you went back in time to the peaceful late Showa Period.

Otsuka Park

Walking twelve minutes south, near the Shin-Otsuka Station, you will find yourself in this relatively small park. Let's take a break here and observe the statue of a young boy performing gymnastics (or being apprehended, depending on how you choose to see it). According to some people, the rajio taiso (radio calisthenics) gatherings that were organized here starting in 1929 were the first in the country, although the Sakuma Park and the Miyagawa Square, both in Chiyoda Ward, are also competing for the same title. Speaking of rajio taiso, it is still broadcasted on NHK (Japan Broadcasting Corporation) every morning.

Gokoku-ji Temple

After you have rested sufficiently in the park, it is time to continue walking southwest until you reach the magnificent 17th century Gokoku-ji Temple. It was built in 1681 and has survived all the earthquakes and wars to date, giving us a rather unique opportunity to view an important Buddhist temple from the Edo Period. By the way, Okuma Shigenobu, a prominent politician and the founder of Waseda University, and field marshal Yamagata Aritomo are both buried here.

Ueno

Where is Ueno?

Located in Bunkyo Ward, Ueno is the cultural, historical and academic center of Tokyo. It came into existence in 1948 after being home to many samurai houses in the Edo Period followed by universities and military zones in the Meiji Period. Mori Ogai, Natsume Soseki, Higuchi Ichiyo, and Ishikawa Takuboku all lived here just to name a few very well-known and influential authors.

It is no exaggeration to say that Bunkyo Ward was the birthplace of modern Japanese literature. It is currently home to a large number of artists, reporters, editors, and scientists.

It takes 26 minutes to get here from Shinjuku Station on the Yamanote Line (200 yen). It is also accessible on foot, but not recommended as it takes an hour and 40 minutes (that is, unless you are prepared to walk much more after that).

Ueno Station

There really isn't anything to explore at the station, with the possible exception of the giant statue of a panda locked inside a transparent plastic box. So, after getting a glimpse of the statue, you should make your way out of the building as soon as possible and visit the Ameyoko shopping street. It is always quite busy, but you will surely appreciate the old-time charm of this neighborhood. Besides the various street foods such as fish and fruits (make sure that you check out *Hyakkaen* fruit store), you can also enjoy many traditional Japanese performing arts such as rakugo (comical story-telling). For rakugo, comedy, acrobatics, and much more, visit the most historic entertainment hall in Tokyo: *Suzumoto Engeijo.*

Suzumoto Engeijo

Address: Suzumoto Bldg. 3F, Ueno 2-7-12, Taito-ku, Tokyo
Phone: +81-3-3834-5906

Other recommendations include *Kadokura*, a bar/restaurant with amazing hamukatsu (ham cutlet), and *Usagiya*, a shinise (a traditional store that has been run by the same family for many generations) Japanese confectionary, founded in 1913.

Kadokura

Address: Forum-aji Bldg. 1F, Ueno 6-13-1, Taito-ku, Tokyo
Phone: +81- 3-3832-5335
Hours: 11:00-23:00

Usagiya

Address: Ueno 1-10-10, Taito-ku, Tokyo
Phone: +81-3-3831-6195
Hours: 9:00-18:00 (closed Wed)

Ueno Park

Ueno Park is an enormous garden that stretches between Ueno Station and The University of Tokyo. This was the first area to be designated as a park in Japan, with a history dating back to as early as 1873. Originally, it was designed as a garden for the Kanei-ji Temple (built in 1625); however it was transferred to state property after the Meiji Restoration, and then to Tokyo City in 1924. It is the best spot for hanami (see below) since the late Edo Period when hundreds of cherry trees were planted here. About 2 million people visit the park every spring during hanami season to enjoy picnic surrounded by over a thousand blooming cherry trees.

If you are wondering about the statue near the southern entrance of the park, it depicts Saigo Takamori, a 19th century warrior and politician, and it was unveiled in 1898. The dog on his right was his beloved Samoyed, Tsun, and they are on their way to a rabbit hunt. Saigo was one of the Three Great Nobles who contributed to the overthrow of the Tokugawa Shogunate and the start of the Meiji Restoration in order to transform Japan into a more open and modern country. The park is open between 05:00 and 23:00 and free to enter. It is right next to the Ueno Station.

Hanami

Hanami is around late March and to early May (depending on the region) and it literally means "flower viewing." It is by far the most magical season in Japan (the second is momiji, the season of autumn leaves). During hanami, nearly everyone living in the country goes to the parks that have cherry trees (or "sakura" in Japanese) to enjoy the stunning views along with food and lots of alcohol. In fact, most of the time, they are more interested in the consumption part than in the flower viewing. There is even a Japanese proverb "Hana yori dango" (rice dumplings over flowers) to express this sentiment. The blue plastic mats lying around the park need to be reserved well ahead in time, especially if you are planning a picnic with a bigger group of friends or co-workers. Otherwise, you can always find an unoccupied patch of grass for yourself or a couple of people to lie down and simply take in the beauty of the flowers.

Ueno Zoological Gardens

Ueno Zoo was established in 1882 and considered to be the earliest zoological garden in Japan. Emperor Showa later presented the zoo to Tokyo City in 1924. In 1972, a giant panda was added to the zoo family in order to celebrate the reparation of diplomatic relations between Japan and China. It currently houses about 400 species and 3000 animals. In the Eastern Park, there are giant pandas (Lili and Shinshin, who arrived in 2011), gorillas, tigers, bears, and seals. In the Western Park, you can see giraffes, hippos, rhinos, aye-ayes, shoebills, as well as amphibians and reptiles. It is open between 9:30 and 17:00 (closed Mon), and the entrance fee is 600 yen for adults (online booking required).

For a change of pace, visit Yanaka, around 15-minute walk north from Ueno Zoo, where you can experience the rustic charm and nostalgia of the old Shitamachi atmosphere.

Tokyo National Museum

The Tokyo National Museum was also the very first of its kind in Japan. So many firsts, I know... but as I said, this is the historical center of Tokyo. The museum opened in 1872 and moved to Ueno Park in 1882. It is the home to 87 pieces of national treasure and 633 important cultural properties (115,653 artworks in total plus 2,519 consigned items). Among these, 200-300 pieces are usually open to viewing. The museum complex consists of six separate buildings, among which Hon-kan (the main building), Hyokei-kan, and Kuroda Memorial Hall have the most impressive appearance.

Hon-kan (completed in 1938) is one of the best examples of Japanese-Western hybrid architecture. This building exhibits objects of art from the ancient Jomon Period to the 19th century, including Buddhist statues, tea ceremony artifacts, samurai equipment, folding screen & sliding door paintings, noh and kabuki masks, ukiyo-e prints, swords, and ceramics. Hyokei-kan is the oldest building of the museum, opened in 1909 to honor the wedding of Crown Prince Taisho. It went through repair work in 2006 and 2007 to restore the interiors.

The construction of the Kuroda Memorial Hall began at the bequest of a Western-style painter, Kuroda Seiki, whose paintings and other artistic endeavors are displayed here. The building was completed in 1928 and opened its doors in 1930 as the home of The Institute of Arts Research for the Imperial Academy of Fine Arts.

Although the rest of the buildings are less impressive from the outside, their exhibitions may still be worth a visit. The Toyo-kan, which features art and historical collections from all over Asia, including Korea, China, Southeast and Central Asia, India, and Egypt, has an impressive collection as well.

The admission fee to the Tokyo National Museum is 620 yen for adults and 410 yen for university students (except for the Kuroda Memorial Hall, which is free to enter). The exhibitions are open between 9:30 and 17:00.

Kuromon

This architectural piece is also a part of the museum and the name means "Black Gate." It used to be at the residence of the Ikeda feudal family. Considering the style and the materials used, it was probably built in the late Edo Period. It was moved near the museum in 1954 from the Crown Prince's villa. Another similarly famous feudal residence gate is at The University of Tokyo, called Akamon, or "Red Gate".

Shinobazu Pond

This pond is located on the southwest side of the park and it represents the Biwa-ko Lake, the biggest inland body of water in Japan (in Shiga Prefecture). On a semi-island within Shinobazu, there is Benten-do, a small Buddhist hall of worship built in the 17th century as part of the Kanei-ji Temple. It is dedicated to Benten (or Benzaiten) the goddess of wisdom and fortune (Sarasvati in the Hindu religion).

Shinobazu Pond can be divided into three sections: Lotus Pond with its countless lotus plants in the summer; Boat Pond, where you can rent a rowboat or a paddleboat; and Cormorant Pond, for bird lovers. The pond is especially lovely at night after all the other visitors have left. In fact, if you are staying nearby, you should go out for a run around midnight, so long as you do not mind occasional encounters with bats and homeless people.

The University of Tokyo Hongo Campus

You can easily walk here from Ueno through the park (29 minutes). There is no direct train or metro connection. The University of Tokyo is Japan's most prestigious university (Tokyo Daigaku, or Todai in short). It regularly comes in one of the top spots in the rankings by Times Higher Education. Its history dates all the way back to 1684 when Tenmonkata, an astronomical institution, was founded. Other predecessors are the Otamaga-ike Vaccination Institution from 1858 and the Shoheizaka Academy from 1790. In 1877, the first two were merged into The University of Tokyo. The two main campuses are the Hongo Campus in Bunkyo Ward, which is mainly used for research and specialized education, and the Komaba Campus in Shibuya Ward, for general education and liberal arts. The number of Nobel laureates affiliated with the university is 8, only slightly behind Kyoto University.

What to see in the Hongo Campus?

The school has eight gates in total, among which Akamon or Red Gate is the most famous and worth a visit. It was originally built in 1827 for the Maeda clan and has since been associated with the university. You will see dozens of junior high and high school students posing for photographs in front of the gate, so just try to squeeze yourself through the crowd and enter the campus. Now you can imagine how annoying it can be to go to classes there every day; no wonder that most of the students do not actually use this entrance.

You should turn left and then right to get to the General Library. The original brick building from 1892 was destroyed in the 1923 Great Kanto Earthquake. The current building was built through a donation from the Rockefeller Foundation and designed by a Japanese architect, Uchida Yoshikazu.

The front side looks like a bookshelf with books lining up. Strangely enough, I had not noticed this until recently. Inside, you will see a red carpet over the stairs as well as gorgeous Western-style interior with chandeliers and paintings. To visit, you will need to complete a short administrative procedure between 9:00 and 17:00.

Faculty of Law & Letters Buildings 1, 2, and 3 were designed by Uchida Yoshikazu and completed in the 20's and the 30's after the Great Kanto Earthquake. Personally, my favorite parts of this complex are the arches that allow you to look through all three buildings if you stand on the northern side of the library. These arches have carvings similar to those used in ancient Greece, which are one of the main characteristics of the distinctive style called "Uchida Gothic".

If you are here in autumn, spend some time on the road that leads from the Main Gate to the Yasuda Auditorium, between the Faculty of Law & Letters Buildings 1 and 2. The fan-shaped leaves of the gingko trees ("ginnan" in Japanese) on this street often paint everything yellow (although they do smell kind of bad), and they can be found in the logo of the university. If you are hungry or you feel like having a beer, you can visit the underground cafeteria in Building 2 for some reasonably priced food and drinks. It is open from 11:00 to 20:00 except for weekends and national holidays.

The perfect place to finish our tour at Todai is the small park with a pond in the middle, just next to the General Library. The surrounding area became a garden in 1638 for the Maeda clan and the lake was originally called Shinji-ike, as its shape is reminiscent of the Chinese character "kokoro" (or "shin"). Later, it was renamed Sanshiro-ike due to influence from Natsume Soseki's novel, *Sanshiro*, in which the pond serves as the location for the main character's first encounter with a girl with whom he falls in love.

May Festival

The festival was first held in 1923 and has been organized almost every year since then. Currently, over 500 groups participate annually, and their job is to entertain the over 150 thousand visitors. The groups cook or bake food, serve drinks, do various performances, or show you what they have been up to since last year's festival. It is definitely an interesting experience, especially if you want to know more about the local students and their lives.

Admittedly, I studied at Todai, so I am a little bit partial, but I am sure you will appreciate the atmosphere this campus has to offer if you choose to visit it.

Ochanomizu

It is just a 16-minute walk from the Akamon to the area called Ochanomizu, or "tea water" in Japanese, a name referencing the Kanda River that flows across the neighborhood. From the Ochanomizu Bridge, you have a wonderful view of the station and the passengers as they wait for the train to arrive. The rails run on the edge of a cliff that follows the river. In front, you will be able to observe another passage over the water, Hijiri Bridge, which was built in 1928. If you come here at night, you will see its beautifully lit arch reflecting on the river, forming a circle. If you keep walking down the main street (the JR station should be on your left), you will find yourself in the largest collection of second-hand musical instruments and ski/snowboard equipment shops.

One of my favorite places to eat here is *Naples no Shitamachi Shokudo*, which serves delicious Italian food in a splendid ambience.

Naples no Shitamachi Shokudo
Address: New Surugadai Bldg. B1F, Kanda Surugadai 2-1-45, Chiyoda-ku, Tokyo
Phone: +81-3-3291-3601
Hours: 11:00-22:00

Tokyo Dome City

It is a 15-minute walk to the west along the river until Tokyo Dome City, a huge entertainment complex with an amusement park, a stadium for baseball and concerts (Tokyo Dome), restaurants, and shops. The Big O, a giant Ferris wheel, provides the visitors with an exceptional view of the area for 850 yen. You can even choose the background music for your 15 minutes ride! By the way, this is the world's biggest center-less wheel with its 60-meter diameter. The Thunder Dolphin rollercoaster, the largest of its kind in Tokyo, passes through the center of the wheel.

Korakuen

Finally, I believe it is time to rest a little bit in the Koishikawa Korakuen Garden, which can be reached within 2 minutes from the Tokyo Dome City. It is a very successful mix of Japanese and Chinese garden techniques, where the plum season (mid February through March), the hanami season (late March to mid May), and the momiji season (late November and early December) are all equally enjoyable. Look for the red Tsutenkyo Bridge!

Akihabara & Asakusa

>> ———————————— <<

The history of "autumn leaf field"

One station away on the Yamanote Line from Ueno (3 minutes, 140 yen) or a 18-minute walk straight south – Welcome to the otaku mecca, Akihabara (or Akiba, in short)! Literally, the name means "autumn leaf field." There are many unknown details about the actual history of this name, although the gist of it can be summarized as follows: There was a big fire in 1869 and the disaster destroyed about 1,100 houses. In fact, such fires were so frequent at the time that

Edo, the capital back then, was even called the "City of Fires". Thus, they decided to leave the current area of Akihabara empty for fire-fighting purposes. Later on, as an added measure against fires, they built Chinka-jinja (fire prevention shrine) here. The people, however, believed that it was the shrine of Akiha Daigongen, the most prominent god of fire prevention, thus they began to call it Akiha-jinja, and after a while the area itself was known as Akihano-hara, Akihaga-hara, or Akihappara. The name stayed inconsistent until the local station started to accept passenger trains as well as cargo trains, when the name "Akihabara" stuck.

Electric Town

Despite the general opinion on the area, Akihabara is not only for geeks (or otakus in Japanese). Virtually anyone living in our modern society can probably find something of interest at Akihabara. This is because, besides all the otaku stores you may encounter here (more details on that in a moment), you can also find the world's largest selection of cheap but still extremely high-quality electronics such as cameras, TVs, computers, vacuum cleaners, and basically anything you can imagine, as well as quite a few things that you probably never even conceived of.

The colossal Yodobashi Camera store, which has become a symbolic building of Akihabara, is right at the Central Gate of the station. Yodobashi Camera was founded in 1960, and as the name suggests, it used to exclusively sell cameras and photography-related products. Since then, it has developed into one of Japan's representative establishments that sells all sorts of electronic items (to be precise, the 5th biggest in terms of sales after Yamada Denki, Bic Camera, Edion, and K's Holdings). Currently, it has 23 shops nation-wide, and Yodobashi Akiba is the second biggest among them (the biggest one is in Umeda, Osaka). The staff has detailed and extensive knowledge about every single product and many of them speak English as well, so feel free to ask them any question you may have about whatever you are looking for. It also has collectible figures and cards on the 6th floor, as well as a golf practice range and batting cages on the 9th floor. The store hours are from 9:30 to 22:00, while the golf range and batting cages are open between 10:30 and 22:00.

If you are not satisfied with the prices you get at this store, don't give up: there are a million and one other places you can visit, such as Sofmap, Yamada Denki, and Llaox.

Duty-free stores such as AKKY are also an option, as some of the items sold in other stores may be designed for use within Japan only. However, if you choose to shop at a duty-free store, please keep in mind the following requirements: you must show your passport, you must purchase over the amount of 5,000 yen, and you must have arrived in Japan less than 6 months before your purchase.

Between the station and Chuo-dori (central street), there is the Akihabara Radio Center, where the Akihabara "Electric Town" began in 1945. After World War II, electronics and radio engineers gathered here in an attempt to sell radio parts and other electronic junk. There are currently 38 tiny retailers in the center selling all sorts of cables, plugs, wires, measuring instruments, switches, lights, and other electronic components. If you are into DIY or you need specific pieces for a device you already own, this is where you should go.

Geek Capital

The other half of Akihabara consists of cafes and shops targeting fans of games, animes, and mangas, as well as the subcultures of J-pop and kawaii. You might be familiar with these concepts already, and if not, I recommend looking into them before sightseeing to have an idea of what to expect. The worldwide market of Japanese manga, anime, and game is a several hundred billion dollar industry. It is quite usual for a manga become an anime, a TV show, or a movie (or, more often than not, a combination of these), then be made into video games, and bring with it a slew of card games (we all remember Pokémon cards, right?), collectible figures, and other goods. Akihabara is absolutely worth a visit, even if you are not completely obsessed with any of these phenomena as it provides a unique opportunity to get totally immersed in (or possibly drown in) a very prominent aspect of modern Japanese culture.

Anime/Manga

Mandarake is an 8-floor building full of items related to anime, manga, cosplay, and so on, close to the Denkigai Gate of the station (hours: 12:00-20:00). Don't forget to check out their floor of customizable dolls, especially if it has been a while since you have had nightmares. They have an online store as well where you may find additional items.

Tamashii Nations is a store that sells toys, figures, and other merchandise by the famous Japanese toymaker Bandai. If you're familiar with any Japanese shows or games, you're sure to find something of interest here.

Tamashii Nations Tokyo
Address: HULIC & New AKIHABARA B1F-2F, 4-4-2 Sotokanda, Chiyoda-ku, Tokyo
Phone: +81-98-993-6093
Hours: 12:00-20:00 (weekday), 10:00-20:00 (weekend)

On June 23, 2022, *Tamashii Nations* will be at a new location at Kanda Hanaokacho 1-1 where *Gundam Café* used to be. *Gundam Café* was a very interesting place dedicated to the Mobile Suit Gundam anime series, but sadly it closed in early 2022, likely due to the pandemic.

Toys/Games

For second-hand collectibles, look for *Liberty*, which owns several stores scattered in Akihabara that are generally open between 11:00 and 20:00. Check out their website for more information (http://www.liberty-kaitori.com/).

For serious collectors of nostalgic TV and computer games, your best bet is *Super Potato*, although it may sound more like a grocery store (general hours: 11:00-20:00). If you find their prices too high, you can always go back to *Mandarake*, as they also sell games (general hours: 11:00-20:00).

After an exhausting day of hunting, have a beer at *A-Button*, where you can enjoy the retro arcade atmosphere while playing old-school games with your friend or a local.

Game Bar A-Button
Address: 5th Kosei Bldg. 1F, Taito 1-13-9, Taito-ku, Tokyo
Phone: +81-3-5856-5475
Hours: 20:00-4:00

Maid Cafés

You are about to enter possibly the strangest world of Akihabara, where the waitresses (or waiters, depending on your inclination) are dressed up in various costumes and literally ready to serve you. This includes waiting on your table, but for some extra fee, you can play rock-paper-scissors with them (be careful, there might be punishment for the loser!), or get spoon fed, and receive grooming, as well as massages. The general rule is that taking photos is absolutely prohibited, unless you can make an agreement with someone, for an extra fee of course. Shinobazu Café is one where the girls are dressed as ninja warriors.

Shinobazu Café

Address: Tsuchiya Bldg. 2F-4F, Soto-Kanda 1-2-3, Chiyoda-ku, Tokyo
Phone: +81-3-6260-8313
Hours: 16:00-21:00 (Tue-Fri), 13:00-21:00 (weekend)

Tsundere, the latest trend in maid cafés, was influenced by animes such as *Kimi ga Nozomu Eien* where the girls are unpredictable, cold and quite mean, although they can become rather clingy after a while.

Unfortunately, the only exclusive tsundere-type maid café has recently closed. That being said, you might still be able to catch an event at *Pinafore* (for more details, visit: http://pinafore.jp/en or their Facebook page).

Animal Cafés

Who wouldn't like to pet cats or rabbits while lingering over a cup of coffee? If you are not allergic to animals, give them a try (and an occasional belly rub)!

Neko Jalala
Address: Suehiro-cho Heim 1F, Soto-Kanda 3-5-5, Chiyoda-ku, Tokyo
Phone: +81-3-3258-2525
Hours: 12:00-20:00 (closed on Thursday)

Remarks: Kitties! 530 yen / 30 minutes + drinks

Bunny Cafe Moff Rell
Address: Saison Akihabara 2F, Soto-Kanda 4-8-3, Chiyoda-ku, Tokyo
Phone: +81 3-3254-2323
Hours: 13:00-20:00 (Tue-Fri), 11:00-19:00 (weekend)

Remarks: Bunnies! 1,100 yen / 30 min or 1,600 yen / 60 min (includes one drink and rabbit food)

J-Pop

If you mix J-Pop with Akihabara, you get AKB48, a popular girl band. As the name suggests, it originally started with 48 members, but by 2014, their number had increased to 140. As of 2022, there are 83 active members. Not surprisingly, their locations are full of middle-aged men in suits, as there is only one thing that is harder to resist for Japanese salarymen (businessmen) than underage girls singing and jumping around in cute uniforms, and that is there being even more of them doing so at once. If you also share their obsession or would like to see salarymen in their natural habitat, visit the *AKB48 café/shop* or the *AKB48 Theater* on the 8th floor of the discount retailer, *Don Quijote*.

Don Quijote
Address: Soto-Kanda 4-3-3, Chiyoda-ku, Tokyo
Phone: +81-570-024-511
Hours: 24/7

Sadly, the AKB48 café/shop closed at the end of 2019 due to railway renovations in the area and as of now there is no plan to reopen. For more information, check out their official website at: https://www.akb48.co.jp

If this is still not enough, at *Dear Stage* you can watch amateur pop idol performances live.

Dear Stage

Address: Dempa Bldg., Soto-Kanda 3-10-9, Chiyoda-ku, Tokyo

Phone: +81-3-5207-9181

Hours: 18:00-22:00 (weekdays), 17:00-22:00 (weekends and national holidays)

Remarks: 3 performances daily on weekdays and 4 performances on weekends and holidays. The entrance fee is 1,000 yen and includes one drink. https://dearstage.com

Asakusa

How is Asakusa different from Akihabara? In every possible way! Asakusa is one of the best-preserved examples of how the city looked like in the post-war Showa era. At the same time, it can be considered a miniature version of Kyoto with its ryokans (Japanese-style inns), jinrikishas (rickshaws), and geishas (Japanese hostesses). Take the Tsukuba Express train from Akihabara, which will bring you here in 15 minutes for 210 yen.

Where did the name of Asakusa come from? Nobody knows for sure, but it may have originated from the Ainu language (where a similar word means "crossing the sea"), the Tibetan language (where a similar word means "sacred land"), or standard Japanese (where it means "shallow grass").

When should you come here?

The best times may be during the Sanja Festival (or Sanja Matsuri in Japanese) in May, the Asakusa Samba Carnival in September, or the Hagoita Market in December.

Sanja (literally "three gods") Festival came into being in 1872 when three separate events merged into one. It is the annual festival of the Asakusa Shrine and one of the most representative events in Japan. During the three days over which it is organized, as many as 30 groups of men, women, and children carry around their own mikoshis (portable shrines). There are also floating stages on which you can witness musicians playing on flutes and drums, as well as dancers. Follow them to the shrine to watch the performance of the Binzasara Mai traditional dance.

Asakusa Samba Carnival was first organized in 1981 and since then it has become the largest Samba contest on the northern hemisphere. Teams gather from all over the country to compete in two leagues!

Hagoita is a wooden paddle used with hane (shuttle) as a set to play hanetsuki, a traditional Japanese New Year's game that bears great resemblance to badminton. At this annual market on Nakamise-dori (see below), you will find hagoitas decorated with kabuki actors and charming Edo ladies. Even

Harry Potter or the former Prime Minister, Koizumi Junichiro, can sometimes show up in these illustrations.

Buddhism and Shintoism in Asakusa

Senso-ji Temple and Asakusa Shrine are the main sites of Asakusa and they are right next to each other. Senso-ji Temple was built in 645 after three fishermen found a statue of Kannon (the goddess of mercy in Buddhism) in Sumida River. These three founders are enshrined in the Asakusa Shrine (completed in 1649), which became a separate entity after the 1868 Shinbutsu Bunri (Separation of Shintoism and Buddhism) decree. The outer gate of the temple-shrine hybrid is called Kaminari-mon ("Thunder Gate") and can be recognized by the giant lantern with the gate's name on it, the two Shinto statues on the sides (Fujin, the god of wind, and Raijin, the god of thunder), the beautiful red color, and a large crowd of people struggling to take photos under the lantern. Beyond this gate is Nakamise-dori, a shopping street stuffed with souvenirs and traditional food stands, leading all the way to the second gate, Hozo-mon. Entering through this gate, we are welcomed by the main hall of Senso-ji and a five storied pagoda. Both of them are reconstructions of the originals that were destroyed in the Great Tokyo Air Raid, but they are nevertheless fascinating especially at night. The shrine is just a few steps from here toward the left.

Let's try the Buddhist fortune-telling ("omikuji") here. Find a stand full of drawers. After inserting 100 yen into the slot below (no cheating), pick up the metal box, shake it well, then read the number on the metal stick that comes out of it. Find the drawer corresponding to your number and take one of the sheets of paper inside. It is usually only written in Japanese, but I am sure you can find someone to translate it for you. Good luck!

Tokyo Skytree

Opened in 2012 as a broadcasting tower, with its impressive 634-meters height, this is currently the tallest tower in the world, and the second tallest man-made structure (right after Burj Khalifa at 829.8 m). It is also surrounded by restaurants, offices, and shopping facilities, forming the Tokyo Skytree Town. The highest observation floor is at 451.2 meters on the 445th floor, which is currently the 4th highest in the world. From here, you have a perfect 360 degrees view of the capital.

You can buy tickets to go up to the 350-meter observation floor (Tembo Deck) or the 450-meter observation floor (Tembo Galleria), or purchase a combo ticket for both. Ticket price ranges from around 1,000 to 3,400 yen depending on the day and the ticket type. The decks are open between

10:00 and 21:00 (the last entry is at 20:00). There is also a café and a restaurant on the 350-meter deck, but it will cost a pretty penny to eat or drink there. Visit their website for the latest information (https://www.tokyo-skytree.jp/en/ticket).

Asakusa Engei Hall

The history of this place goes back to 1907 with a movie theater called Sanyu-kan. After the war, in 1951, its site was turned into Furansu-za, a striptease theater, but the organizers shut this down in 1964 and started the Toyo Theater, where, for instance, Kitano "Beat" Takeshi was one of the actors. I am sure you remember him from *Hana-bi* or from *Zatoichi*. On the 4th and 5th floors of the same building, they opened Asakusa Engei Hall in 1964, which has since moved to the ground floor. Besides rakugo (comic monologue storytelling), they also have manzai (traditional stand-up comedy), and other genres. It costs 2,800 yen (2,300 yen for students) to enter and you can stay until closing time.

Foooood

Asakusa is mainly known for its yakitori (fried chicken) and tempura (other deep-fried things), so I will recommend a restaurant/bar from each of these categories. *Daikokuya Tempura* was established in 1887 and is especially famous for its tendon (tempura rice bowl).

Daikokuya Tempura

Address: Asakusa 1-38-10, Taito-ku, Tokyo
Phone: +81-3-3844-1111
Hours: 11:10-20:30 (weekdays & Sunday), 11:30-21:00 (Saturday & national holidays)

Asakusa Toriyoshi

Address: Asakusa 1-8-2, Taito-ku, Tokyo
Phone: +81-3-3844-6262
Hours: Lunch is 11:30-14:00, and dinner is 17:00-22:00 (Sunday 11:30-15:00 and 17:00-21:00)

Ginza

>>> ———————————— <<<

Short introduction of Ginza

This is the ultimate shopping district with expensive luxury goods, fancy bars/lounges, lavish hostess clubs, and art galleries. It was originally the location of the feudal government's silver molding and issuing agency back in the Edo Period ("gin" means "silver"). You can get here from Asakusa by taking the Ginza Metro Line (19 min, 200 yen). Even if you are not keen to spend all your life savings, Ginza still has many things to offer that are free or relatively cheap.

Walking around Ginza

The Ginza Chuo-dori (central street) was the first place in Tokyo to implement the Pedestrian's Paradise rule in 1970, allowing people to walk on the road without having to worry about cars or bikes on weekends and national holidays from 12:00 to 18:00 (April-September) or 12:00 to 17:00 (October-March). Akihabara and Shinjuku followed Ginza's example, although with a more limited schedule. While wandering on Chuo-dori, pay attention to some of the unique architectural pieces such as the *Mikimoto Boutique, Ginza Wako*, and the *De Beers* building, which looks a bit like the Dancing House in Prague.

Mikimoto was founded in 1893 by Mikimoto Kokichi, a Japanese inventor, who was one of the first creators of cultivated pearls (although the actual method was patented to Nishikawa Tokishi and Mise Tatsuhei). His company enabled Japan's pearl business to skyrocket and reach a production of 10 million pieces a year. *Mikimoto Boutique* focuses on casual jewelry, and the building itself is worth a look with its irregular glowing windows.

Wako is a department store famous for its main building in Ginza at the crossing of Chuo-dori and Harumi-dori. Its predecessor was *K. Hattori*, a retail shop selling imported watches and jewelry since 1881 (now Seiko Holdings

Corporation). Since then, the clock tower has become the symbol of Ginza and is featured in many movies, including two Godzilla motion pictures. The current neo-renaissance building was completed in 1932 after the Great Kanto Earthquake. At every hour, the Westminster Chimes are played from the tower.

Window shopping is another popular activity in Ginza, where no display can be too weird. Have a look at *Mitsukoshi*, *Matsuya*, and *Tokyu Hands*. The last one is a must-see from the inside as well, particularly for DIY fans, but the large selection of odd items guarantees a fun time for everyone.

If you have not seen a kabuki play before, this might be your best chance, as one of the best theaters in Japan happens to be in Ginza. Kabuki-za Theater opened in 1889, although it has been rebuilt and renovated several times since then. It can accommodate almost 2,000 visitors and the tickets are rather affordable.

Ginza turns extraordinarily magical at night when the streets become colorful canvases due to the hundreds and hundreds of neon signs.

Eating in Ginza

For lunch, I recommend *Ginza Sushidokoro Marui*, where you can have a filling rice bowl-style sushi meal with soup included.

Ginza Sushidokoro Marui

Address: Ginza 3-8-15, Chuo-ku, Tokyo
Phone: +81-3-3564-8601
Hours: 11:30-14:30 (lunch), 16:00-21:00 (dinner)

For dinner, why not visit one of the restaurants of the trendy "Oreno" series (literally "my [something]"), which serves gourmet food at affordable prices? Unless you cannot stand the idea of standing throughout your meal and having a 2 hours limit for your stay, you will surely be satisfied with *Oreno Italian*. If you definitely want to sit down, reserve early!

Oreno Italian Tokyo

Address: Kirarito Ginza B1F, Ginza 1-8-19, Chuo-ku, Tokyo
Phone: +81-3-5579-9915
Hours: 12:00-1500 & 17:00-20:00 (weekdays), 12:00-23:00 (Sat), 12:00-22:00 (Sun)

I know I said I was not going to discuss anything expensive here, but I just cannot skip *Sukiyabashi Jiro*. This restaurant has received a 3-star rank from the Michelin Guide 8 years in a row and was the subject of the 2011 documentary, *Jiro Dreams of Sushi*. Quality of course comes with a price: it costs 30,000 yen to have a meal here and you need to reserve your seat at least a month ahead.

Hibiya

A 7-minute walk on the Harumi-dori toward the Imperial Palace will take us to Hibiya, a neighborhood between Hibiya Park and Yurakucho. This area is the birthplace of Toho Company, a major Japanese filmmaker and distributor. On the northern side of the shopping mall *Hibiya Chanter*, look for the tiny Godzilla statue. This square is also covered with the handprints of famous movie stars.

Hibiya Park is a perfectly relaxing place to have a picnic or to pick up a book and lie down somewhere near the fountain.

Yurakucho

If you are still looking for something to eat or drink, just head toward the elevated tracks of the Yamanote Line in either direction from Yurakucho. You will find a countless number of bars and restaurants on both sides of the rails. This kind of area is called "gado-shita" or "under the girders". Yurakucho is also known for its convention and exhibition center, the Tokyo International Forum, which consists of several halls, a museum, a restaurant, and many other facilities. Hall A is the second largest concert hall in the world with its capacity to seat 5,012 people (after Radio City Music Hall of New York). The ship-themed Glass Hall is also worth seeing.

Tsukiji Market

Only 5 minutes from Hibiya on the Hibiya Metro Line (170 yen), this was the home to the largest fish market in the world (in terms of money transaction; the Ota Market actually has a larger surface area). Its history goes back to the 1930's when it first opened. In a typical year, the transactions in the market amounted to about 900,000 tons and 6 hundred billion yen.

The Tsukiji Market was made up of an inside and an outside area. The tuna auction and the wholesale market, which were the most popular attractions, took place in the inner market. The tuna auction allowed a limited number of visitors who usually arrived before 5:00 each day to apply for entry at the Osakana Fukyu Center near the Kachidoki Gate. The wholesale market area could be accessed by the public only after around 10:00 when most of the business had been conducted. There are also many restaurants both inside and outside the building.

In October, 2018, the inner market moved to a new location in Toyosu, around 4 km south. The outer market (now called Tsukiji Outer Market) is still open to the public and you can buy various kinds of food and other goods here.

At the new Toyosu Market, the tuna auction starts at 5:30 and continues until around 7:00. As before, plan to arrive before 5:00 when the doors open to visitors and spectators. Be sure to check online for updated entry restrictions due to the pandemic (https://www.shijou.metro.tokyo.lg.jp/english/).

When going to either market, it is recommended not to bring big suitcases, children, or pets, and to always be careful not to block the traffic. Have a fresh sushi breakfast or lunch while you are there!

Imperial Palace

The Imperial Palace

This was formerly the location of Edo Castle, the residence of Tokugawa shoguns between 1603 and 1867. Edo Castle was renamed as Tokyo Castle in 1868 when Emperor Meiji visited from Kyoto and began the Meiji Restoration. The next year, in 1869, it was renamed again as Imperial Castle, and in 1888, the construction of the Meiji Palace was completed, but it was destroyed in 1945 in air raids. In 1948, the area ceased to be referred to as "castle" and instead as "Kokyo" or "Imperial Residence" (although in English its official name is still the "Imperial Palace"). In 1968, construction of a new palace was completed and is currently being used for formal events. Their Majesties the Emperor and the Empress are living in a building in Kokyo named "Gosho." Kokyo's postal code is 100-0001 and its total area including the surrounding parks adds up to 1,150,000 km^2. The Imperial Palace (Kokyo) consists of four main areas: the inner grounds, the East Gardens, the Outer Gardens, and Kitanomaru Park (where you'll find the Nippon Budokan, the Science Museum, and the National Museum of Modern Art).

From the Outer Gardens, you can see a double-arched stone bridge, the Seimon-ishibashi ("main gate stone bridge"). Seimon-tetsubashi ("main gate iron bridge") is right behind it. It is also known as Niju-bashi (double or two-fold bridge) because it had two levels until 1964 when the wooden structure was changed to iron.

The inner grounds of the palace are closed to the public except on the 2nd of January (New Year's Greeting) and the 23rd of February (the Emperor's Birthday). You can also join a 75-minute tour that guides you around the imperial grounds if you make a reservation ahead of time. The Imperial East Gardens are generally open to all visitors besides Mondays,

Fridays, and special occasions. If you look around carefully, you can find old ruins of Edo Castle here.

Sannomaru Shozokan, the personal art collection of Emperor Hirohito (also known as Emperor Showa) is in this garden, exhibiting gorgeous kimonos and paintings. The moat next to Kitanomaru Park is Chidoriga-fuchi, which is another popular spot to observe the cherry blossoms. Heading south from here, you will see the giant building of the National Theatre of Japan in front of you next to the Sakurada Moat, where you can watch noh, kabuki, or kyogen (short, comic intermission between noh acts) performances.

Immediately southeast of the palace grounds are Marunouchi and Nihombashi, business and financial districts where you'll find the headquarters of the country's largest banks as well as the Tokyo Stock Exchange. In Marunouchi, *Tokyo Station Gallery* and *Mitsubishi Ichigokan Museum* are certainly worth visiting. Look out for Nihombashi Bridge after which the area was named!

The Imperial Palace has been and is still effectively the very center of Tokyo as well as Japan. First Edo Castle, then Meiji Palace, then finally the National Diet Building and the Tokyo Station served this function. It is an ideal place for jogging and enjoying the rare greenery and fresh air in the middle of the sprawling metropolis.

Nippon Budokan

The Nippon Budokan, or Budokan for short, was originally built to house the judo competitions of the 1964 Tokyo Olympics. The designer Yamada Mamoru used the octagon shaped Yume-dono building of the Horyu-ji Temple (Nara Prefecture) as reference. The ridged lines of the main roof symbolize Mount Fuji. Since then, it has been operating as a multi-function venue for many events and activities including martial arts, combat sports, dance competitions, concerts, and university entrance and graduation ceremonies. The first foreigner to perform at Budokan was the conductor Leopold Stokowski in 1965. He was followed by The Beatles in 1966, Led Zeppelin in 1971, Deep Purple in 1972 and 1973, and Queen in 1975, just to mention a few of the legendary artists that graced its stage. If you do not mind sharing the experience with 10 thousand other fans, get tickets for the next gig!

Yasukuni Shrine

The shrine is easily accessible from Budokan: just cross the moat on the north and then turn left. Its predecessor was the Tokyo Shokon-sha from 1869 that changed its name to Yasukuni in 1879. Its main purpose was to comfort the spirits of the people who sacrificed their honorable lives for the nation since 1853 in times of national crisis such as the Japanese-Sino War, the Japanese-Russo War, and the Pacific Theater of World War II. Currently about 2 and a half million spirits are enshrined here, including many war criminals.

Besides the two main events of the Spring Festival and the Autumn Festival, there is Hokyu-shiki on the 15th of August, the day when Emperor Showa announced Japan's surrender in a live radio broadcast in 1945. As the name suggests, the highlight of the ceremony is setting dozens of doves free.

If you want to know the exact time when cherry blossoms begin in Tokyo, look for the representative sakura tree near the shrine, which is used to pronounce the official opening of the hanami season by the Japan Meteorological Agency.

Other sites of interest include the statues of animals, the statue of a war widow with her children, and the statue of a kamikaze pilot, as well as Yushukan, a museum that displays materials from World War II such as personal possessions, documents, and weapons. Admission is between 9:00 and 16:30 and costs 800 yen (500 yen for university students). The shrine gardens are generally open from 6:00 to 17:00 (or later depending on the month).

Jimbocho

This area towards the north of the palace can be reached within 15 minutes on foot. Jimbocho has the highest density of bookstores in all of Tokyo, especially when it comes to old, second-hand prints. They also have a big selection of English and photo/picture books.

Kanda

Another 18 minutes walk north-east across the Sumida River will bring you to Kanda Myojin Shrine (or take the Shinjuku Metro Line to Awajicho and walk straight north for about 12 minutes), the home of the famous Kanda Festival, which is considered to be one of the three largest traditional matsuri (festivals) in Japan (the other two are Gion Matsuri in Kyoto and Tenjin Matsuri in Osaka). An extravagant version is held every other year (odd-numbered years) in mid-May, while the scale is considerably smaller in the other years. It is certainly an unforgettable sight to witness about 300 Edokkos (people who were born and raised in the Kanda area, the city center during the Edo Period) marching through the main streets carrying some 100 portable shrines on their shoulders. If you miss it or if you want to know more about history of the festival, visit the Kanda Myojin Museum in the same area as the shrine (hours: 10:00-16:00, fee: 300 yen for adults).

The shrine itself was originally built in 730 and even though it has been reconstructed and renovated several time since then, the current buildings are still able to provide you with an amazing atmosphere. Due to its proximity to Akihabara, it is frequently visited by people who need divine protection of their digital devices. You need not miss out either: take home a charm (omamori) to shield your gadgets from malicious forces (1,000 yen).

Yushima Seido, formerly Shoheizaka Academy, is also nearby, so why not take visit and also take a look at the world's largest Confucius statue there?

On the way to Kanda Myojin, or on the way back, visit the Holy Resurrection Cathedral (or Nikolai-do in Japanese), the main cathedral of the Japanese Orthodox Church. It was completed in 1891 and has survived both the Great Kanto Earthquake and the Great Tokyo Air Raid with only minor damages. If you go between 13:00 and 15:00, you can enter for a 300 yen donation at the entrance.

I am sure you feel hungry by now, so head back to Awajicho once again, where they have been serving the highest quality soba (buckwheat noodles) for more than a 100 years. Both of the following sell mainly "yabu" (rough) soba.

Kanda Yabu Soba

Address: Kanda Awaji-cho 2-10, Chiyoda-ku, Tokyo
Phone: +81-3-3251-0287
Hours: 11:30-20:30 (closed on Wednesdays)
Remarks: It was founded in 1880.

Kanda Matsuya

Address: Kanda Suda-cho 1-13, Chiyoda-ku, Tokyo
Phone: +81-3-3251-1556
Hours: 11:00-20:30 (Mon-Fri), 11:00-19:30 (Sat and national holidays). Closed on Sundays.
Remarks: It was founded in 1884.

For an astonishing tea and Japanese confectionery experience, visit *Takemura*.

Takemura
Address: Kanda Suda-cho 1-19, Chiyoda-ku, Tokyo
Phone: +81-3-3251-2328
Hours: 11:00-20:00 (closed on Sun and Mon)
Remarks: It was founded in 1930.

Tokyo Station

This is the center of Tokyo's, and in fact all of Japan's, train network, and a 20-minute walk from Awajicho or a 3-minute metro ride on the Marunouchi Metro Line (170 yen). The first plans for the station were made at the end of the 19th century when an intermediate station became necessary to connect Ueno and Shimbashi stations. The fascinating red brick building was completed in 1914 and currently has the largest number of platforms in Japan including those for train, metro, and the shinkansen (bullet train).

The station itself is full of intriguing historical elements. For example, on the platform of the 6th track (Yamanote Line, Tohoku Keihin Line towards Shinagawa Station) you can find a green, thick support pillar that has been here since the very beginning. After this, let's go to either the 4th or the 5th track platforms, from where we can observe a bronze post with a zero on the top of it. This particular piece was installed in 1969 and shows the beginning of the Yamanote Line.

By the way, did you know that two prime ministers have been assassinated at this station? One of them was Hara Takashi, who was stabbed by a station employee (from a different station) in 1921, and the other one was Hamaguchi Osara, who was shot by a right wing group member in 1930 and died a year later from the infected wound.

Japan Rail Pass

You might consider buying a Japan Rail Pass that will allow you to travel freely on any JR trains, buses, most of the shinkansens, and one ferry line (JR-WEST Miyajima Ferry that runs between Miyajimaguchi, Hatsukaichi, Hiroshima, and Miyajima-Itsukushima). On the condition that you are a temporary visitor with permanent foreign residency, you can order your pass before your visit and then pick it up in Japan. There are two types of passes: the green for first-class cars, and the regular pass. Both passes are available for 7, 14 or 21 consecutive days starting on the first day of use, depending on your choice. Your best bet is probably the ordinary 21-day pass for around 60 thousand yen, as three weeks are absolutely necessary if you want to travel around Japan and see most of the sites. Visit their website for details (https://japanrailpass.net/en/).

Roppongi

A few things about Roppongi

You should learn a little bit about the history of Roppongi before you head out with your friends to party all night long. It used to be a land of samurai residences and later named Roppongi-cho, which was a monzen-machi (a neighborhood formed around a famous temple or shrine). Two main theories exist about the origin of the name "Roppongi", which literally means six trees. One of them attributes it to six pine trees that were planted around here. The other one sounds more compelling, as it interprets the name in an abstract fashion and connects it with the names of the six feudal lords who lived here and had a tree-related Chinese character in their names: Aoki, Hitotsuyanagi, Uesugi, Katagiri, Kutsuki, and Takagi. Since the collapse of the Japanese bubble economy at the end of the 80's and the beginning of the so-called Two Lost Decades, the disco's here have morphed into karaoke bars and kyabakuras. Kyabakura is a made-up word from cabaret and club, and they are similar to hostess bars, where you pay a certain amount per hour for a lady ("kyabakura-jo") to attend to you, serve you alcohol, and keep you company. Currently Roppongi is home to many embassies (Spanish, Swedish, etc.), US military facilities, clubs, illegal casinos (gambling is prohibited in Japan except for betting on a handful of sports), drug trafficking, organized crime, and some foreign mafia. Nevertheless, it is still a very safe place by international standards, and, if you are careful, nothing could happen to you or your possessions.

How to get here? Take the Marunouchi Metro Line from Tokyo Station to Ginza Station, then change to the Hibiya Metro Line and get off at Roppongi Station.

Tokyo Midtown

First of all, let's go to Tokyo Midtown. It is connected underground with the station, so just follow the signs (5 minutes). It is basically like Sunshine City with shops, offices, mansions, a hotel, a hospital, and a park. It was completed in 2007. The park area frequently becomes a venue for various lively events such as gourmet or liquor nights, so check their schedule before you go.

Nogi Shrine

This is a 7-minute walk from Tokyo Midtown.

General Nogi Maresuke, an important figure in the Japanese-Russo war, and his wife, Shizuko, are enshrined here. They committed suicide at their home on the day of Emperor Meiji's funeral (September 13, 1912) as atonement for all the lost lives (57,780 soldiers dead or wounded) in the Siege of Port Arthur. The shrine, standing very close to his original apartment, was built in 1923, and then rebuilt in 1983. The couple and both of their sons, who died during the war, are buried at the Aoyama Cemetery close-by (another 7 minutes walk). This was the first publicly owned cemetery, originally built in 1872. Hachiko, the famous dog I mentioned in the Shibuya chapter, also rests here with his beloved owner.

Roppongi Hills

Your next destination should be Roppongi Hills (12 minutes by walk from Aoyama Cemetery or 15 minutes from Nogi Shrine). It is another complex similar to Tokyo Midtown, but much more impressive. It opened in 2003 with the 54-story high Mori Tower in its center, and the tower is quite enjoyable on its own.

On the 52nd floor of the tower, you can find The Sun & The Moon, a café and restaurant hybrid. There is also an indoor observation deck (Tokyo City View) and the Mori Arts Center Gallery. It has a spectacular view of the city during both the day and the night. Tokyo City View is open from 10:00 to 22:00 every day. It costs 1,800 yen to enter (1,500 yen if you buy it prior at a convenience store; 1,200 yen for university students). From here, you can also access the Sky Deck, which is an observation deck on the roof (the hours are 10:00-20:00 and the fee is an additional 500 yen). Check their website for updated schedule as it does change from time to time (https://tcv.roppongihills.com/en/). The Sky Deck is also the venue for occasional DJ events, large-scale Halloween parties, as well as the Roppongi Astronomy Club. This club holds star-gazing events and seminars/workshops every month and it is free to join them! Check out their webpage (https://tcv.roppongihills.com/en/tenmon/).

The 53rd floor houses the Mori Art Museum, which regularly holds exhibitions of contemporary art, photographs and architecture. It is open from 10:00 to 22:00 (Tuesdays 10:00-17:00) and costs 1,800 yen (1,200 yen for students). You are also allowed to enter Tokyo City View with the same ticket.

If you feel like reading something, visit the 49th floor, which has Academy Hills, a seminar/conference center with its own library.

Besides these, there are also several offices (TV Asahi, Lenovo Japan, J-WAVE commercial radio, GREE, etc.), and shops, of course. And this was only Mori Tower. Let's see what else Roppongi Hills has to offer:

Toho Cinemas Roppongi Hills offers a luxurious experience with reclining leather seats (Screen 7, +3,000 yen fee). The regular rate is 1,900 yen per adult. I would recommend going on the 1st of the month or on a Wednesday since a movie costs only 1,200 yen on those days. By the way, every weekend, they have movies until 5:00 in the morning.

Mori Garden, just east of Roppongi Hills, is a gorgeous 4,300 square-meter garden with a lake, a waterfall, a river, and many, many sakura and gingko trees. It is open every day between 7:00 and 23:00. Its extraordinary design, which began in 1650, lets you observe all fours seasons of Japan.

The Maman (French for "mother") spider is a bronze, stainless steel, and marble sculpture by Louise Bourgeois at the base of Mori Tower. Look for the sac, which contains 26 marble eggs. You can also find a similar spider in Bilbao, Seoul, London, and Ottawa. Its name comes from the fact that the artist dedicated this piece to her mother, Josephine.

After all this sightseeing, it is time for some traditional ramen.

Afuri Roppongi Hills

Address: Metro Hat / Hollywood Plaza B2F, Roppongi 6-4-1, Minato-ku, Tokyo
Phone: +81-3-3408-1880
Hours: 11:00-23:00

Clubs and other weird places

Get a can of *Ukon no Chikara* (sort of tumeric mixed into a sugary drink) before the long night. It will likely save you from a bad hangover. Another rule about clubbing in Japan: you have to be at least 20 years old, so don't forget your ID!

You would think that Roppongi is stuffed with great dance clubs, but unfortunately this is not the case anymore. Most of them have closed, although I did manage to find some.

V2 TOKYO (formerly ELE TOKYO)

This is a large club with two floors and a basement. The basement is mostly VIP area, although VIP tables are on each floor (reserve beforehand). The music depends on the night, and it varies from hip-hop through trance to techno and house.

Address: Tower of Vabel 1F/B1F, Roppongi 7-13-7, Minato-ku, Tokyo
Phone: +81-3-5474-0091
Hours: 21:00-05:00

Remarks: Free entry for ladies and 2-10,000 yen for men depending on day and event (https://www.v2tokyo.com)

If you do not find *V2 TOKYO* satisfying, people seem to recommend *Bonobo* or *Womb* in Shibuya. There used to be a gigantic club called *ageHa* in Shin-Kiba, but it closed down in January, 2022, due to lease expiry after 20 years. *Bonobo* is a house that has been renovated into a club and offers a cozy atmosphere not found in most other places... not recommended if you happen to be claustrophobic!

Bonobo

Address: Jingumae 2-23-4, Shibuya-ku, Tokyo
Phone: +81-3-6804-5542
Hours: 21:00-05:00 (Tue-Thu), 22:00-06:00 (Fri-Sat), 17:00-23:55 (Sun), closed on Mon
Remarks: Entry fee from 1,500 to 2,000 yen depending on the event (includes one drink)

Womb

Address: 1F, Maruyama-cho 2-16, Shibuya-ku, Tokyo
Phone: +81-3-5459-0039
Hours: 22:00-04:30
Remarks: Costs 2-4,000 yen to enter.

If you decide to stay in Roppongi, you might be interested to explore the region's bizarre selection of BDSM dungeons. For beginners, the soft S&M bar *Blackrose* is advisable. The thrill-seekers should head to *Jail* or *Sugar Heel*...

Blackrose

Address: Yamanaka Kasumi-cho Bldg. 6F, Nishi-Azabu 3-24-19, Mina- to-ku, Tokyo
Phone: +81-3-5843-1019
Hours: 21:00-03:00 (weekdays only)
Remarks: 8,000 yen for entry. Funnily enough, this place is categorized as a wine bar on some websites.

Jail S&M and Fetish Bar

Address: Imperial Roppongi No.1 2F, Roppongi 5-16-5, Minato-ku, Tokyo

Phone: +81-3-5544-9958

Hours: 21:00-03:00

Remarks: Entry 10,000 yen for visitor, 5,000 for member (for membership, register on their app), price may change for special events (for more information: https://jail.tokyo/en/)

Sugar Heel

Address: 144 Bldg. 3F, Roppongi 4-12-5, Minato-ku, Tokyo

Phone: +81-3-5410-1550

Hours: 20:00-01:00 (closed on Sun and national holidays)

Remarks: For men, it costs 10,000 yen / hour (only the first drink is included). For women, it is only 1,000 until closing time. For couples, it is 12,000 yen until midnight and 6,000 yen / 30 minutes after midnight.

After a long night of dancing or being whipped, you should get some drunchies (drunk munchies) at a late-night diner such as *Café Eight*.

Café Eight

Address: Court Annex Roppongi 2F, Nishiazabu 3-2-13,
Minato-ku, Tokyo
Phone: +81-3-5414-5708
Hours: 24/7

Another option is of course the nearby 24/7 McDonald's at
Roppongi 6-3-1 (most likely the largest McDonald's in Tokyo)
where you may find menu items exclusive to Japan!

Grab a bite or pick up some take-out and walk toward Tokyo
Tower on the Gaien Higashi-dori. It takes 20 minutes on foot
to get there and it is utterly gorgeous at sunrise. Of course, it
is also beautiful at night, which you have probably already
confirmed yourself from Roppongi Hills. Tokyo Tower, the
333 meters tall structure, was built in 1958 and since then
has become one of the symbols of the capital.

If you still have enough stamina in you to continue (sleep is
for the weak!), catch the Hibiya Line metro at the Kamiya-cho
Station until Kasumigaseki, then change to Chiyoda Metro
Line until you reach Akasaka Station. It should not take you
more than 21 minutes. Have a cup of espresso and a snack
at the cozy *Tokyo Little House* while browsing the selection
of books there, and recharge for the next day.

Tokyo Little House

Address: Akasaka 3-6-12, Minato-ku, Tokyo

Phone: +81-3-3583-0228

Hours: 11:00-17:00 (weekdays only)

While you are here, you should visit the Akasaka Palace, one of the two State Guesthouses of the Japanese government. It was originally designed to serve as the Imperial Palace for the Crown Prince when it was built in 1909. You need to apply in advance to gain admission, but trust me it is worth it.

On the way back to the station, finish the day with a dinner at *Ninja Akasaka*, where the staff is (obviously) dressed in ninja outfits and will also perform various ninja tricks for you if you are lucky.

Ninja Akasaka

Address: Akasaka Tokyu Plaza 1F, Nagata-cho 2-14-3, Chiyoda-ku, Tokyo

Phone: +81-3-5157-3936

Hours: 17:00-20:00 (weekdays), 11:30-14:30 and 17:00-22:00 (weekends)

Tokyo Bay

>> ———————— <<

This is our last area in Tokyo, although technically some parts belong to Chiba Prefecture. As it is quite large, it might take 2-3 days to cover everything, especially if you are planning to visit Tokyo Disney Resort and other theme parks.

Shinagawa

Walking here from Akasaka or Roppongi might take too long, so I recommend that you take the Chiyoda Metro Line from Akasaka until Hibiya, and then change to JR Keihin Tohoku Line at the Yurakucho Station (26 minutes, 330 yen). This station is one of the biggest hubs of the Japanese railway system that connects Tokyo with Northern, Southern, and Western Japan, as well as with Narita and Haneda airports. It started operating in 1872 and immediately became a part of the Shimbashi-Yokohama line. In 2002, they installed a monument on the platform of the 5th and the 6th tracks celebrating the 130th year since its opening. This station had a key function in rearranging the metropolitan infrastructure to prepare for the Tokyo Olympics. This is also the station where the state-of-the-art maglev train, Chuo Shinkansen, will connect Tokyo with Nagoya (planned for 2027 but since then postponed, 40 minutes) and with Osaka (planned for 2037, 67 minutes). The technology enables the train to reach a 505 km/hour speed (during testing, it reached 603 km/hour, which made it the fastest train in the world).

Just outside the station, have a bowl of ramen on Shinatatsu Ramen Street, then head to Mita Station via Keikyuu Main Line / Asakusa Metro Line (they are virtually the same line, so you do not need to change anywhere).

Keio University Mita Campus

Five minutes from the station you will find yourself at Keio University, the most prestigious and highest ranking private university in Japan. It was founded in 1858 as a Rangaku-juku (a private school where Japanese people could learn Western academics). Moreover, the founder was Fukuzawa Yukichi, a liberal ideologist, writer, and teacher who was one of the most influential figures in modern Japanese history. He is actually the person on the 10 thousand yen banknote. We can consider him to have been the Benjamin Franklin, the Voltaire, and the Mustafa Kemal Atatürk of Japan.

Why is this campus worth a visit? Here, you can see the first auditorium of Japan, the Mita Auditorium, which was built in 1875 with the construction funded entirely by Fukuzawa's own money. Although the original design was influenced by Western architecture, it also exhibits the typical Japanese tile-roofed wooden structure and Namako walls (white grid pattern on black slate).

Fukuzawa believed that public speech and debate were extremely important, thus he was the one who translated and introduced these concepts to Japan for the first time. You must not miss the historical library building either. It was built in 1907 to honor the 30th anniversary of the university. Its gothic appearance, along with its red brick and granite material, makes it a truly impressive structure. The building is open between 8:45 and 21:50 (weekdays) or 8:45 and 17:50 (Saturdays).

Shimbashi

Shimbashi is a 37-minute walk along the bay or a 4-minute ride on the Asakusa Metro Line (180 yen) from Mita Station by Keio University, and it is the ultimate salarymen paradise as it is equipped with an abundance of offices and gado-shita style small bars (just like in Yurakucho). Shimbashi Station was the first train station in the history of Japan, connecting Tokyo with Yokohama in 1872. You should visit the Railway History Exhibition Hall that holds artifacts and photographs related to the history of this area where the first trains were running. It is open between 10:00 and 17:00 (closed on Monday) and free to enter.

The first gay bar after World War II, "Yanagi" opened here, serving such famous customers as Alain Delon, Yves Saint-Laurent, and Pierre Cardin. It closed in 1989, but currently there are numerous related locations in this area to choose from, making Shimbashi the 3rd biggest gay district in Tokyo (after Shinjuku and Ueno/Asakusa). Among these, *Town House Tokyo* should be highlighted.

Town House Tokyo (gay bar)

Address: Le Glacier Building No.36 5F, Shimbashi 3-8-6, Minato-ku, Tokyo
Phone: +81-3-6435-6988
Hours: 17:00-1:00 (Tue-Thu), 15:00-23:00 (Sat-Sun), closed on Mon and national holidays
Remarks: It has karaoke (free on weekends), cheap drinks, and regular underwear-only nights. Visit their website for more information (http://townhousetokyo.com/).

You should expect a more mature atmosphere here compared to the Shinjuku LGBT scene.

For the ladies, regrettably there are not very many options around Shimbashi, as most of the women-only bars seem to cluster around Shinjuku 2-chome (or ni-chome). The most popular among these seem to be *Dorobune* and *Adezakura*.

Dorobune Lesbian Bar

Address: Vera Heights Shinjuku Gyoen, Shinjuku 2-7-3, Shinjuku-ku, Tokyo
Phone: +81-3-3356-3358
Hours: 19:00-00:00 (Tue-Thu, Sun), 19:00-01:00 (Fri-Sat), closed on Mon and national holidays

Adezakura

Address: Shinta Building 1F, Shinjuku 2-15-11, Shinjuku-ku, Tokyo
Phone: +81-3-3351-4833
Hours: 21:00-05:00, closed on Tue
Remarks: No entry fee and most drinks are 900 yen, women only until after around 1 a.m.

There is also *Agit* right next to *Adezakura* if you'd like to try a slightly different and maybe a bit more traditional experience of a Japanese girl bar, complete with karaoke machines!

Tokyo Disney Resort

From Shimbashi Station, take the JR Yamanote Line to Yurakucho Station (3 min, 140 yen), walk to Tokyo Station, then get on the JR Keiyo Line to Maihama (16 min, 220 yen).

Tokyo Disney Resort is composed of two theme parks, Tokyo Disneyland and Tokyo DisneySea. The former is the first Disney amusement park to open outside of the USA in 1983. Disney Sea was added later in 2001.

Tokyo Disneyland has the 2nd largest number of visitors in a year (within amusement parks / theme parks) after the Magic Kingdom in Florida. It is made up of seven themed lands. Try their jalapeno & cheese popcorn!

Tokyo DisneySea is the first Disney park with a water/sea theme. Originally, this park was supposed to be built at Long Beach (Los Angeles), but the local municipality did not agree to the plans. Like Tokyo Disneyland, this park also has seven themed ports. It targets a more mature audience by serving alcohol and offering gourmet menus. One recommendation is *Ristorante Di Canaletto* in the Mediterranean Harbor. It is not only aesthetically pleasing from inside and outside, but if you sit on the terrace, you can enjoy the view of sliding gondolas in the canal in front of you as if you were in Venice!

There are plenty of reliable websites that can help you plan your trip down to the last detail, but I can give you a few pieces of information. There is no single ticket for both of the parks, so you need to buy them individually. The actual price will depend on whether you go at daytime or only in the evening. I do recommend DisneySea over Disneyland as it is indeed a unique experience you cannot find elsewhere.

Odaiba

To reach Odaiba, go back to Shimbashi from where you should take the Yurikamome Line to Odaiba-kaihinkoen Station (13 min, 330 yen). Yurikamome Line is a monorail service that provides you with an amazing view of Tokyo Bay and many sites on the way such as the Rainbow Bridge,

Tokyo Tower, Tokyo Skytree, and Tokyo Gate Bridge. There will be several bold architectural pieces as well: the Fuji TV Building, the Telecom Center, and the Tokyo Big Sight. The last one is also known as Tokyo International Exhibition Center and is home to the Tokyo International Anime Fair, the Comiket Comic Fair, and the Tokyo Motor Show.

What is Odaiba exactly? It literally means fort, which is not a coincidence. After Commodore Perry came to Japan to negotiate a trade agreement in 1853, the government decided to build eleven forts near the shore with cannons. These were called Shinagawa-Daiba or Odaiba. In the end, none of them were used and Japan peacefully opened its harbors to the West. Later on, the bay saw the creation of a dozen or so artificial islands as an attempt to expand the metropolis. One island was named Odaiba as a memento of the historical forts, of which the 3rd and the 6th still exist nearby.

Get off at Odaiba-kaihinkoen Station for Decks Tokyo Beach where you can get lost among over 3 million Lego bricks at *Legoland Discovery Center*, in virtual-reality games at *Tokyo Joypolis*, or simply in the gorgeous view of Tokyo Bay.

Legoland Discovery Center

Address: Deck Tokyo Beach Island Mall 3F, Daiba 1-6-1

Hours: 10:00-16:00 (closed Tue and Wed)

Fee: 2,250-2,800 yen depending on the time and whether you buy it there or online

Tokyo Joypolis

Address: Deck Tokyo Beach 3F-5F, Daiba 1-6-1

Hours: 11:00-19:00 (weekday), 10:00-20:00 (weekend)

Fee: Admission and rides cost 3,500-4,500 yen for adults & 2,500-3,500 yen for children (7 to 17 years old) depending on your time of visit. For admission only, it costs 800 yen for adults & 500 for children.

The Odaiba Statue of Liberty, a replica of the French sculpture, was installed near Odaiba Seaside Park (Kaihin-koen) in 2000 due to popular demand after the French original stood there from 1998 to 1999 in commemoration of the "French Year in Japan."

From here, you can walk directly to Aqua City Odaiba, where you should sit in at Kua'aina for a perfect Hawaiian burger. DiverCity Tokyo Plaza with its life-sized Gundam robot is also just a few steps away.

Kua'aina

Address: Aqua City Odaiba 4F, Daiba 1-7-1, Minato-ku
Phone: +81-3-3599-2800
Hours: 11:00-22:00

Walk south along the Yurikamome Line for 12 minutes to reach the Museum of Maritime Science. It is easy to notice as the main building looks like a giant cruise ship. If you are a water person, you will love it. They are open from 10:30 until 16:00 and the admission is free.

Walk for 14 more minutes along the rails and you will be at Telecom Center Station where you can check out the National Museum of Emerging Science and Innovation. You will find hands-on exhibits and classes exploring the future of science & technology, plus a cafe and a gift shop. Hours are 10:00 to 17:00 (closed on Tue) and costs 630 yen for adults and 210 yen for children (up to age 18).

Cruise on the Sumida River

Take the Yurikamome Line back to Hinode Station (13 min, 330 yen) where you can change to the Tokyo Water Bus at Hinode Pier just north of the station. For only 860 yen, off you go to Asakusa on the Sumida River (40 minutes). Otsukaresama, you have explored most of Tokyo!

Yokohama

Yokohama, about 30-40 km south of Tokyo, is the second most populated city in Japan with 3.8 million people. It functions as one of the main harbors of Japan and used to be the center of international trade and transportation for several decades after it opened to the world in 1859. It is a popular place to visit for Tokyo citizens as well due to its intriguing history and proximity to the sea.

First of all, you should get to Yokohama Chinatown as early as possible. From Asakusa, take the Asakusa Metro Line, which will turn into Keikyu Main Line after 11 stations, to arrive at Yokohama Station. Here, change to the Minatomirai Line then get off at Motomachi-Chukagai Station. The entire trip takes 50 minutes and costs 820 yen.

Yokohama Chinatown

This is one of the three Chinatowns in Japan (the others are in Kobe and Nagasaki) and considered to be the largest one in Japan and also in Asia, with over 500 shops in an area as small as 0.2 square-kilometers. Its history goes back to 1855 and there are more than 6,000 Chinese people living here. If you happen to be here in February, make sure to visit the neighborhood during the Chinese New Year celebrations. They usually have parades and traditional Chinese performances with lion and dragon heads.

In order to enter, you need to pass through one of the four main gates of the district. Inside, you will find five more gates and the colorful temple of Kanteibyo (or Kuan Ti Miao), which was built in 1873 to honor Kuan Ti, the god of fortune and fbusiness. Try the street food here including ramen noodles, dumplings, steamed buns... *Kocho* allegedly has the best steamed buns (nikuman in Japanese) in the area.

Kocho

Address: Yamashita-cho 138-24, Naka-ku, Yokohama-shi

Phone: +81-50-5484-9830 & +81-120-290-892

Hours: 11:00-15:00 & 17:00-22:00 (Mon-Fri), 11:00-22:00 (Sat, Sun, and national holidays)

Find a tapioca seller and walk around while sipping on it. You will realize that people-watching in Yokohama Chinatown can be quite a fun activity on its own.

Motomachi

After Chinatown, you should walk south to reach the old foreign district of Motomachi. March would be a perfect time to be here as they annually hold a large-scale sale on the Motomachi Shopping Street, called "Charming Sale." If you are not interested in shopping, make your way toward the Yokohama Foreign General Cemetery, where you can enter a small section with approximately 4,200 graves in it. It is only open to the public on weekends and national holidays in exchange for a 200-300 yen donation. Wander on the hills of Motomachi and you might be able to discover some historical Western-style houses.

Minatomirai

From Motomachi-Chukagai, take the Minatomirai Line again and get off at the Minatomirai Station (4 min, 190 yen), which is located in the district of Minato Mirai 21. This name was chosen from submissions from the public in 1981 and it reflects the desire of the locals to make Yokohama a "harbor city of the future 21st century." There are many things to see here, so let's look at them one by one.

Yokohama Landmark Tower is a shopping, hotel, and office complex completed in 1993 and used to be Japan's tallest skyscraper until 2014 (now it is Abeno Harukas). Go up to the Sky Garden on the 69th floor on Japan's fastest elevator (750 m/min) and enjoy the beautiful view of Yokohama. It is open from 10:00 to 21:00 (22:00 on Sat) and the admission fee is 1,000 yen.

In front of Landmark Tower, you will see the Nippon Maru sailboat, a part of the Nippon Maru Memorial Park. The boat was built in 1930 and its main function was to train sailors. During its approximately 54 years of activity, it traveled 45.4 times the earth's circumference and raised 11,500 sailors. Imagine yourself as one of these sailors and explore each floor and corner of the ship (10:00-17:00, 600 yen)!

The Yokohama Cosmo World amusement park was originally built for the Yokohama Exotic Showcase (YES in short) '89, but it has continued to operate since. Cross the water to the artificial island where the Cosmo Clock 21 stands, the biggest digital clock (Citizen, of course) embedded Ferris wheel in the world. For 900 yen, you can observe the entire bay area including the Landmark Tower. The ride takes about 15 minutes.

If you walk to the other side of the island, the Yokohama Red Brick Warehouse will appear in front of you. The two sections were built as customs buildings in the beginning of the 20th century. Currently, various interesting events and exhibitions are organized both inside and outside.

You may also be able to catch some nice fireworks by the water, especially in the summer, which are best watched from the nearby Osanbashi Pier with a beer in your hand.

When it is nearing late afternoon, walk back towards Cosmo Clock 21 until you reach Yokohama World Porters. Here, choose from one of the restaurants by the water, you won't regret it. After enjoying your dinner at sunset, the most stunning view on the area is offered by the Yamashita Park, which is 12 minutes away by walk. Absolutely breathtaking, isn't it? While you're there, take a look at the Girl Scout Statue and the Hikawa Maru ocean liner from 1929.

At the end of the day, how about staying in a hotel that looks at Minato Mirai 21? Navios Yokohama, which is right on the artificial island, offers plenty of rooms like that for 6-10 thousand yen a night. Just remember to reserve ahead on Jalan.net.

Southern Yokohama

Next morning, hop on the number 8 bus at Nihon-Odori Station just across the water to the south. It will take you to Sankei-en Garden in around 30 minutes. This traditional Japanese-style garden was designed by Hara Sankei (real name Hara Tomitaro), a wealthy businessman trading in silk, and opened in 1906. Have a cup of tea surrounded by historical feudal lord residences, ponds, and a three-story pagoda (9:00-17:00, 700 yen).

From Sannotani (bus stop), catch bus number 101 or 58 to the Negishi Station, where you need to get on the JR Negishi Line until Shinsugita. Here, you change to Seaside Line and ride the train until Hakkeijima (60 minutes and 700 yen in total). Hakkeijima Sea Paradise opened in 1993 and consists mainly of an aquarium, Aqua Resorts, and an amusement park, Pleasure Land. By the way, Japan seems to have the highest number of aquaria in the world (somewhere between 60 and 70 depending on the source).

The most popular attractions of the Aqua Resorts are the whale sharks (the only ones on display in Eastern Japan) and the "touch and learn lagoon" (Fureai Lagoon), where you can have direct contact with dolphins, penguins, and other marine animals. To visit this and other aquariums, it cost 5,500 yen for an adult for a day-pass. There are other ticket options available (http://www.seaparadise.co.jp/en/price/).

At Pleasure Land, be sure to try Japan's first surf coaster that runs partly above water (1000 yen for a ride)! Check the opening hours before you go. You should also keep in mind that if you want to fully enjoy Hakkeijima Sea Paradise, it might be advisable to set aside an extra day here.

Once you are done splashing around, grab a lunch box somewhere near the station and take the Seaside Line back to Uminokoen-Shibakuchi Station (2 min, 240 yen), or simply walk over in around 7 minutes. From here, walk northwest for about 12 minutes to the Shomyo-ji Temple, which belongs to the Shingon Risshu Buddhist sect and was built around 1258. The strikingly peaceful garden was added in 1320 and later reproduced in 1987. The colors, the silence, and the gently overwhelming feeling of history can make it a perfect location for lunch. It is open between 8:30 and 16:30 for no admission fee.

I hope you are up for a swim (if the season and the weather permit) because you are going to Zushi, which is one of the most popular beaches in eastern Japan. Tattoos have been prohibited since 2014, so hide them well if you have some. From Shomyo-ji Temple, walk for 15 minutes to reach Kanazawa-bunko station, and take the Keikyu Main Line to Zushi-Hayama Station (10 min, 200 yen). From there, it is only an 11-minute walk to the beach. Enjoy!

Kamakura

Kamakura

This is one of Japan's most important religious centers with more than 70 active temples and shrines. Most of them are open daily from 9:00 to 16:00 for 100-300 yen entrance fee. Kamakura was the capital of Japan during the Kamakura Period (1185-1333). In modern times, it was the home of numerous influential writers and artists, who are called

Kamakura-bunshi, such as Akutagawa Ryunosuke and Kawabata Yasunori. Be sure to explore the shores of Sugami Bay, between the Izu and the Miura peninsulas, called the Shonan region. One theory concerning the history of this name attributes it to a former similarity between the Chinese prefecture of Hunan and Kamakura, which were the centers of Zen Buddhism within their countries. The Shonan area has a fun and relaxing atmosphere, similar to California, although with more nature and history. Besides swimming and relaxing, you can also try clam digging (shiohigari), surfing (both summer and winter), or windsurfing. Just be careful, the beach is reserved in late August every year by the jellyfish community.

Take the JR Yokosuka Line from Zushi to Kita-Kamakura Station (12 minutes, 170 yen) or the JR Shonan-Shinjuku Line (13 minutes, 170 yen).

Temples and Shrines

Walk east from the station to Engaku-ji, which was built in 1282 and to this day still houses priests practicing and studying Zen here. Even the public can join their zazen (meditation) sessions on the weekends. It is known for its traditional gardens and gigantic bell from 1301.

Cross to the other side of the rails, where you will find narrow stone stairs in a cedar forest leading up to the Jochi-ji Temple. It is a part of the same branch of Buddhism as Engaku-ji, and was built a year later in 1283. Look for the Nectar Well (Kanrono-ido), which is one of the ten fresh water sources in Kamakura, as well as the three wooden statues of the past, present, and future Buddhas.

Crossing the rails again toward the south-east, you will reach a big green area with Kencho-ji Temple in it, which dates back to 1253. It is the oldest Zen related building in Kamakura and certainly worth a visit, especially for the colorful decoration of Dharma Hall (Hatto) and the beautiful dragon painting on its ceiling. From here, you can take the Tenen Hiking Trail that leads up to Zuisen-ji through forests and hills in about 60-90 minutes. The Zen rock garden here with its flowers and plum trees should not be missed.

After Zuisen-ji, walk west to Tsurugaoka Hachiman-gu Shrine, one of the highlights of Kamakura. It was founded in 1083 and moved to its current location in 1180 by Minamoto Yoritomo, the first shogun of the Kamakura government. The shrine is dedicated to Hachiman, the protecting deity of the Minamoto clan. Personally, my favorite part is the lotus pond with the Taiko (drum) Bridge over it. The pond separates into two sections, the Minamoto side and the Taira (the Minamoto clan's arch enemy) side. The former has three tiny islands, implying "birth", "prosperity," or "creation" (indicating life, with the same pronunciation as the number three) and the latter has four islands, referring to "death" (the same pronunciation as the number four in Japanese).

If you have the time for another brief visit, go to Hokoku-ji Temple towards the southeast across the Shakuji River. It is also called the Bamboo Temple due to its abundant bamboo groves growing inside the garden.

Walk back to Kamakura Station, then walk southwest towards Hase Station (23 minutes) or take the Enoshima Dentetsu Line there (Enoden, in short; 4 minutes, 200 yen). It is said that in the early 40's the train would get so crowded that the windows would break and ten passengers would have to sit inside the washroom to fit into the car. Enoden is by far my favorite train line in Japan, as the view is always unbelievable and the cars are painted happy colors (green or purple). Head north from the station and order a lunch set at *Shamoji*. Try their shirasu (small anchovies or sardines)!

Shamoji

Address: Hase 1-15-2, Kamakura-shi, Kanagawa
Phone: +81-4-6724-5888
Hours: 11:30-15:30 (lunch), 17:00-21:30 (dinner)

It'd be a good idea to hurry now as you do not have much time left before the temples close. Go north towards Kotoku-in, where you can find one of the two most important Buddha statues in Japan. There used to be three of them (in Kyoto, then in Kobe), but the third one was always destroyed one way or another. The other statue is at Todai-ji in Nara, by the way, which I also highly recommend that you visit one day. Both the temple and the 11-meter tall statue are surrounded by mystery and several different theories exist regarding their history. What we know, however, is that if you pay an extra 20 yen, you can see the Buddha from the inside.

The next destination will be the last temple for today unless you would like to walk around a bit more. Hasedera, built in 736 according to the legends, is just a few minutes away from Hase Station. It is famous for an almost 10-meter tall wooden statue of the eleven-faced Kannon, the goddess of mercy, as it is considered to be one of the largest of its kind. Strangely enough, ten out of eleven heads are quite small and they casually stand on top of the main, bigger head.

On the way to the Kannon-do Hall where the aforementioned sculpture is enshrined, you should peek into Jizo-do as well. It contains hundreds of small jizo statues, the patrons of travelers and deceased children. They are recognizable from their adorable faces and occasional red bibs. Be sure to visit the observation deck nearby and enjoy the view while munching on a dango (rice dumplings on a stick with sugar and soy sauce).

On the way back, take a break in the temple garden at the base of the slope where you should see the Benten statue (do you remember the chapter on Ueno?) that was allegedly carved by Kukai himself, the priest who founded the Shingon school of Buddhism.

Before leaving Hase, I would recommend looking around in the local souvenir and handcraft stores, which are great sources of ceramics and washi (Japanese-style paper).

Enoshima

Jump on the next Enoden to Enoshima Station (18 minutes, 260 yen) and walk for about 15 minutes to Enoshima, going across the bridge. This land-tied island is currently inhabited by about 360 citizens and has two caves (Iwaya Caves) as well as steep cliffs on the southern side. The stone plates below offer a perfect location for sunbathing and fishing during low tide. You can also climb the hill to the giant bell where couples attach a lock with their names on it onto the fence after ringing the bell together. This tradition comes from a legend about a love story involving goddess Benten and a reckless five-headed dragon.

If you have 10-15 thousand yen in your pocket (possibly more depending on the season), rent a room in the local ryokan, *Iwamotoro*. Otherwise, you can certainly find cheaper options inland.

Iwamotoro Honkan

Address: Enoshima 2-2-7, Fujisawa, Kanagawa
Phone: +81-466-26-4121

If you decide to stay for the night in Enoshima and the next day falls on a weekend or a national holiday, take a boat back to the mainland in the morning. Remember to bring your camera; you can catch an excellent view of Mount Fuji, which just happens to be your next destination!

Mount Fuji

»» ———————————— ««

The Symbol of Japan

No guidebook about Japan or Tokyo can be complete without mentioning Mount Fuji, which is not only the highest point on the Japanese islands but also the most magnificent view in the entire country. Its imposing presence is due to the year-round snow-capped peak that reaches an impressive 3,776 meters, the gradual inclines that seem to never end, and its visibility from 20 of the 47 prefectures of Japan, reaching about 300 km radius. In 2014, they finally succeeded in taking a photograph of the peak all the way from Kyoto! So, there is no wonder why this mountain is so important for the Japanese.

Mount Fuji is an active stratovolcano that erupted in 1707-8 for the last time. Since the capital moved to Edo in the 17th century, the volcanic cone has been the theme of countless paintings such as Hokusai's *36 Views of Mount Fuji* and Utagawa Hiroshige's work of the same title. Many works of literature have depicted the mountain as well including the remarkable *Manyoshu*, the oldest collection of Japanese poetry. It is told that the first person to ascend was an En no Ozunu, a mystic and ascetic, in 663, and the first foreigner was Sir Rutherford Alcock, in 1868. In 1872, they lifted the ban that prevented women from entering this sacred territory. Nowadays, it is a popular travel location for both Japanese and foreign tourists.

Hakone

On your way to Mount Fuji, I recommend visiting Hakone, a mountainous town known for its hot spring resorts (onsen) and fantastic views of Mount Fuji. Most hotels and inns in the town also offer onsen on-site, so be prepared for a relaxing time soaking in hot water! Besides the hot springs, there are some other sites of interest for you to check out. The *Hakone*

Open-Air Museum has various indoor exhibits as well as an outdoor sculpture park (https://www.hakone-oam.or.jp/en/).

Hakone Open-Air Museum

Address: Ninotaira 1121, Hakone, Ashigarashimo

Phone: +81-460-82-1161

Hours: 09:00-17:00

Remarks: Admission costs 1,600 yen per adult

Lake Ashinoko nearby is worth a visit for the fantastic views of Mount Fuji as well as boat rides on the water. Around the lake, you'll find trails, observation decks, parks, gardens, as well as shrines. Stop by the *Hakone Visitor Center* just north of the lake for more information!

Hakone Visitor Center

Address: Motohakone 164, Hakone, Ashigarashimo

Phone: +81-460-84-9981

Hours: 09:00-17:00 (free entry)

Climbing Mount Fuji

It is time to experience Mount Fuji first-hand! The climbing trails are usually open only between early July and mid-September. You should be well prepared and carry rain and cold protection, a headlamp, and a map, at least. Water, snacks, and trekking boots are also recommended. These are necessary to help you cope with the temperature change (more than 20 degrees Celsius difference compared to the foothills) as well as thunder, lightning, and dense fog. In order to avoid mountain sickness, drink water frequently, rest regularly at locations such as mountain huts, walk slowly at a constant pace, and breathe deeply. All of the four trails are color-coded so be sure to follow your path at the junctions.

The yellow Yoshida Trail starts at 2,300 meters and has zigzag paths (up to the 7th station) as well as slightly rocky ones (5-7 hours for ascent, 3-5 hours for descent). The red Subashiri Trail starts at 2,000 meters and has relatively mild, tree-covered paths (up to the 7th station; 5-8 hours for ascent, 3-5 hours for descent). The green Gotemba Trail begins at 1,450 meters and has gentle slopes with lots of volcanic gravel (up to the 8th station; 7-10 hours for ascent, 3-6 hours for descent). The blue Fujinomiya Trail has the highest altitude at starting point (2,400 meters) and tends to be generally quite steep and rocky (4-7 hours for ascent, 2-4 hours for descent).

The Yoshida and the Fujinomiya trails are the most popular because they have a sufficient number of mountain huts, especially on the way up, as well as first-aid centers. The 10th station denotes the summit for all trails. If you do decide to hike up, definitely avoid going during Obon week (mid-August), because this is the busiest time of the year. If you are experienced enough, you should try to go in early July or early September when there are less student groups, although the weather can be somewhat unpredictable.

If you ask me, I suggest that you climb up until the 7th or 8th station on the first day, take a few hours sleep in one of the mountain huts, and then continue to the summit early morning to see the sunrise. (Don't forget that the sun rises between 4:30 and 5:00 during the summer!) Walk around the crater – this should take you about an hour – then descend.

The Yoshida Trail has the largest number of mountain huts, and it usually costs around 5,500-8,000 yen per night per person (extra 1,000 yen for a meal), although some huts allow you to stay on a per-hour basis (1-2,000 yen per hour). Bring some cash with you even if you do not plan to stay in a hut, as the toilets are generally not free either. Moreover, they will ask for a 1,000 yen donation at the head of each trail (5th station). Visit the official website for climbing Mount Fuji for latest updates (http://www.fujisan-climb.jp/en/).

There are many ways to get to the trails, thus you should look into the transportation options after you have decided which trail to take and when. Have a nice climb!

About Us

Welcome to JpInsiders, home of everything Japanese! If you're interested in the unique culture that this innovative and exciting country has to offer, we can offer you exactly what you're looking for and more.

Here at JpInsiders, we're experts in Japanese culture, and can satisfy your every need no matter what exciting area fascinates you.

Nestled in the heart of East Asia, Japan is home to one of the richest cultures the world has to offer, having pioneered an impressive range of concepts that have gained worldwide traction and popularity.

For example, Japan is the original home of anime and manga, the iconic Japanese cartoons and comic books that millions throughout the world have grown to know and love.

When it comes to the arts, Japan is forever developing new and exciting concepts. A whole host of popular crafts including bonsai, the art of growing miniature versions of trees or shrubs, and the intricate paper craft of origami both originated on Japanese soil.

Over the years, Japanese innovation has truly set a precedent that the rest of the world looks up to.

Whatever your personal interests, we are here to provide you with everything you may need to explore Japan's fascinating culture in greater detail.

We stock a range of books on everything from growing a bonsai tree to learning the Japanese language.

Or how about you get your hands on a great travel guide to help you pinpoint the must-see spots for your next visit?

Whether you are planning a memorable holiday in Japan, wishing to learn a brand-new skill, or simply intrigued by the country's wonderful culture, we will be delighted to help.

Explore our products and get ready to take in all the details you may like to know on Japanese culture.

If you have any question or query, please feel free to get in touch with us for more information. Immerse yourself in all the best and the most up-to-date details on this truly special country with the help of JpInsiders!

PS: Can I Ask You for a Quick Favor?

First of all, thank you for purchasing _Tokyo Travel Guide Insiders_! I know that you could have picked any number of books to read, but you picked this one and for that I am extremely grateful.

If you enjoyed this book and found some benefit in reading it, I'd like to hear from you and hope that you could take some time to post a review on Amazon.

Your feedback and support will help me to greatly improve my writing craft for future projects and make this book even better.

THANKS!

:)

Printed in Great Britain
by Amazon

44207008R00079